anybody's bike book

*This book is dedicated
first to Pat, my love,
and second to the memory
of my dear old Cinelli.*

Acknowledgments

*More than thanks to Pat.
And to Paul Schoelhamer.
Many thanks to those who pitched
in: Dan Nall; Roger, Marcia, and
Don Sands; Phil Shipley, Syd Joselyn,
Kathy Rose, Gary MacDonald,
David Morrison, Jim Houston,
Laurie Karl Schmidtke, Billy Menchine,
Pat & Nancy Heitkam, Michael Ray,
Mark Jansen, and
Glen from New Orleans.*

anybody's bike book

an original manual
of bicycle repairs

newly revised &
expanded edition

written by tom cuthbertson
illustrated by rick morrall

Ten Speed Press

Thanks again Jon Scoville

ANYBODY'S BIKE BOOK is published by
Ten Speed Press, Box 7123, Berkeley, California 94707
© Copyright 1971, 1974, 1976, 1978, and 1979 by Tom Cuthbertson and Philip Wood

Library of Congress Catalog No. 76-29188
ISBN 0-89815-003-5, paper
ISBN 0-89815-004-3, cloth
Beverly Anderson Graphic Design
Printed in The United States of America

Contents

Introduction

This is a book about fixing bicycles. It is written in such a way that anyone can use it to fix any bicycle. Many of you (especially the ladies) have been given the idea that if something is mechanical, you can't do it. That is outrageous. Bicycles are not monstrous machines that only wizards can understand. They are all simple enough that with a little know-how and patience, anyone can work on them. *You can do it!* You don't have to know any magic. The mechanical mystique is a lie.

A bicycle is a wonderful, practical machine, but it is fallible, like any other machine. Any bicycle needs attention. It needs lubrication and adjustment from time to time. It is subject to wear and accidental damage, both of which require repair.

Now, once there was a time when people said, if they had a machine in need of attention, "My, my, I'll have to take that damn machine down and have it attended to." They took the machine to a shop, then went off to a job where they made lots of money to pay for having their machine "attended to."

That wasn't a bad plan. It worked, and still works, for many people. But some people have started doing the whole thing differently. They now say, when their machine needs attention, "Why don't *I* attend to my good old machine, instead of paying someone else to? Instead of spending all my time working for money to pay someone else, I can spend my time learning about and maintaining my own machine."

People are starting to learn just how much they can do for themselves. They are learning to be masters over their machines, instead of slaves to them.

Some machines are harder to master than others. Automobiles, for instance, have a nasty habit of blowing up—a very direct and unpleasant response to a master's attention. Other machines get shorts and shoot sparks at their masters. Because of the nasty habits of these machines, men have learned to cover them up or hide them behind sheet metal and chrome. The machines are therefore hard to get at and attend to.

Consider the bicycle by comparison. No explosives. No sparks. No bothersome sheet metal and chrome to remove. Just the essential machine, sitting out in the open where its master can easily attend to its every need.

If you use this book carefully, always remembering the RULES OF THUMB, and keeping in mind your limitations and the book's (you and I are human, after all, and we are bound to make some mistakes), you can be a proud master over your bicycle.

If you go one step farther, and learn to have fun tinkering with the wonderful intricacies of your bike, who knows where your attentions to your machine will lead.

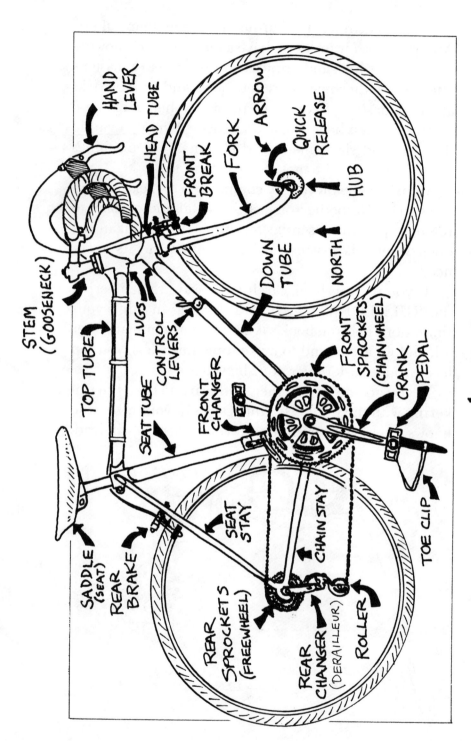

HAND LEVER

HEAD TUBE

STEM (GOOSENECK)

FRONT BREAK

FORK

ARROW

QUICK RELEASE

HUB

DOWN TUBE

NORTH

TOP TUBE

SEAT TUBE

LUGS

CONTROL LEVERS

FRONT CHANGER

FRONT SPROCKETS (CHAINWHEEL)

CRANK

PEDAL

SADDLE (SEAT)

REAR BRAKE

SEAT STAY

CHAIN STAY

REAR SPROCKETS (FREEWHEEL)

REAR CHANGER (DERAILLEUR)

ROLLER

TOE CLIP

Illustration **1** THE BICYCLE

Getting a Bike

Before you buy a bicycle, think about what you are going to use it for. Then look at used bikes as well as new ones that will fit your need. A well-cared-for bike is one of this limited planet's greatest re-cycles!

If you are going to ride over plowed fields, or on sand flats at low tide, or if you plan to take only short rides to the corner store, get a sturdy coaster-brake model, a balloon-tire bomber. Price: two to ten hours work at laborer's wages.

If you plan leisurely shopping jaunts, weekend excursions up to 30 miles, or commuting for short distances, all on reasonably even terrain, get a 3 speed. A good light (25 to 35 lbs.) 3 speed will do just what most of us want and need it to. Price: eight to twenty-five hours work at laborer's wages.

If you plan to cover long distances over varied terrain, and if you are willing to accommodate yourself to a specialized riding position for the sake of vast improvement in cycling speed and responsiveness, get a 10 speed. Price: fifteen to two hundred hours work at laborer's wages, and more if you want to blow it!

There are bikes between and outside these three categories. There are special Bike Moto-X machines, for instance, which can be very costly if they are light and strong. Or for the jet-setter, there's the incredible Bickerton foldable (available from Bickerton Cycles, Ltd., 1314 N.W. Glisan St., Portland, Oregon 97209). If you want to get an unusual or very elegant machine, though, you should consider the difficulty you might have in getting replacement parts.

When you have decided what type of bike you want, shop around and see as many different brands as possible. Remember, as you compare bikes, that the *frame* is the most expensive and significant part. If you buy a bike with a good frame, you can make equipment changes to suit yourself without spending a lot of money. But if you buy a bike with a heavy, weak frame, you are stuck with it. For some specific suggestions and hints, see the *Frame* chapter. The wheels and tires are almost as important as the frame. Get ones that are strong enough to do what you want, but as *light* as possible. There are many possibilities among the standard "clincher" or "wire-on" tires, so avoid the fancy racing "sew-up" or tubular tires unless you race. For more info, see the *Wheels* chapter.

Take any bike you like on a test ride. Ride it up and down hills, around curves, over rough and smooth pavement. If it feels good, buy; if not, don't. And don't be afraid to use color as part of your decision about how you feel. If you like the color of the bike, you'll ride it more and care for it better. I *love* dark blue bikes, for instance. You may like white ones; whatever you like, get.

Be decent to bike dealers, and hope they'll be decent to you. That sounds silly, but I have worked in and been around bike shops for years, and I've seen just how incredibly indecent customers can be. Don't expect a new bike you buy from a shop to be absolutely perfect. Bicycles are made by humans. To err is human. Use this book and it will help you overcome the human element of error. Go through the *Maintenance Checklist* with your new bike and read and follow the chapters on the parts referred to. That will familiarize you with your bike, and this book as well.

If you have trouble with a new bike, ask the dealer nicely if he will help you. Nine times out of ten he will oblige. The fact is, some of the problems you have with your new bike might be due to *your* newness to *it.* You are as human as the people who built the bike. It takes a while for a new rider and a new bike to get acquainted. Give your relationship with your bike a little time and patience, and it will grow into a strong friendship.

Some Rules-of-Thumb

1. For the purposes of this book, the term "left side" means the left side of the bike when you are facing forward on it. The same is true for the term "right side."

2. *On most bolts and nuts, clockwise* (often abbreviated cl) *tightens, counter-clockwise* (abbreviated c-cl) *loosens.* All exceptions to this rule will be noted in the text.

3. Any two parts that screw together have threads. Threads are easy to strip. To avoid stripped threads, first make sure both parts have the same threads, then start screwing the parts together slowly and carefully. Never force two threaded parts to screw together if they resist. And don't tighten bolts and nuts too tight. Remember—the smaller the bolt or nut, the gentler you have to be. When tightening an 8 or 9 mm nut, don't try to demonstrate your virility; show some sensitivity. Threads are delicate.

4. Nine-tenths of the work you do to solve any mechanical problem goes to finding out just where the problem is. If you have a problem and you know generally where it is, before you start dismantling random parts of your bike, use the *Description and Diagnoses* sections in this book to help you get oriented and find the specific trouble.

5. If you ever run across ball bearings that are retained in a round metal clip, don't throw up your hands in despair and confusion. Rejoice; you won't have to chase the bearings around the floor. Just notice, as you take the retainer out, which way it goes back in. Usually, the solid ring side of the retainer goes against the *cone,* and the side with the gaps through which the balls stick goes against the *cup* of a bearing set.

6. Dismantle as little as possible to do any repair. When you do have to take something apart, take it apart slowly. The more time you spend learning about the order of a unit's parts as you dismantle it, the less time you will have to spend reassembling the unit correctly. An old mechanic's trick: spread a clean rag out on your workbench, then put the little parts in rows as you take them off the unit; that'll make it easier to put them back together in the right order.

7. This book isn't about every bike in the world. Your bike may have parts that are different from the ones described and illustrated. Find, in the description of whatever part you are working on, the *most similar* example I use. Use the description which is marked for your type of bike—1, 3, or 10 speed. Each paragraph is marked for the type of bike it refers to; 5 and 15 speed bikes are identical to 10 speeds in all ways except the number of front sprockets (chainwheels).

8. Don't read this book without looking at your bicycle. This is a three-way conversation among you, your bike, and this book; don't leave anybody out. Step by step, do it together.

9. Think before you attack rust-frozen bolts and nuts. Is there any way you can get by without loosening that bolt or nut? Are you going to be able to replace the parts around the frozen bolt or nut if you ruin them? If not, proceed with extreme caution.

Try Liquid Wrench or any other penetrating oil (you can get it at auto parts stores) before you use any tools. After you squirt it on, let it soak in for a few minutes, and maybe give the stuck part a few *light* taps with a hammer to encourage the oil on its way. When you use wrenches, use only ones that fit well. If you have no luck, try to find a place on the bolt where you can saw with a hacksaw without hitting the bike frame. When you have finally loosened or removed the part, promise yourself that you won't leave the bike out in the rain again. Ever.

10. Find a bike shop that *cares.* They will get you hard-to-find parts, give you advice, and help you when this book can't. There *are* bike shops that care. They aren't necessarily the big and flashy ones—remember, it's the people that count. When you find a good shop,

do all your business there. Tell people who want new bikes to shop there. It's the least you can do in exchange for the small-parts hunting that a good shop will do for you.

11. Cultivate a fine ear so you can hear any little complaint your bike makes, like grindy bearings, or kerchunking chain, or a slight clunking of a loose crank. You don't have to talk to your bike when you ride it—just learn to listen to it affectionately.

12. Keep all bearings adjusted properly. Your bicycle has between 150 and 200 ball bearings. To keep them all rolling smoothly, you have to learn to adjust the *cups* and *cones* in which they run. Adjustment involves screwing the cone and cup together until they are snug on the ball bearings, then unscrewing the cup and cone slightly. The bearing should revolve smoothly, without any "play" or looseness between the cup and cone.

Maintenance Checklist

● *The three must-do jobs:* There are three maintenance items that give cyclists more trouble than all others put together; check them before EVERY ride!

Chain: Keep it oiled! On 10 speeds, the same goes for the little rollers the chain goes through on the gear changer. Keep a light film of ten to thirty weight motor oil on the chain, or if you're fastidious, a spray-on dry lubricant.

Tires: Keep them filled to the pressure recommended on the sidewall [see page 107 for a neato check].

Wheels: Can you wiggle them from side to side with your fingers when the bike is standing still? If so, either the big nuts or the quick-release levers are loose (tighten them *now*) or the bearings need adjustment [see chapter 7].

- *Other things to check:*

Grease and oil: Any bearings on a bicycle which are packed with grease (wheel, headset, bottom bracket, pedal) will stay lubricated, under normal conditions, for six months or more. Any bearings which are left out in the rain or covered with sand will stay lubricated about six days. If your bearings are greased (most are), keep them out of the rain and don't oil them. Overhaul and grease them once or twice a year, then leave them alone. Use a high-grade bike grease, like Lubriplate or Phil Wood waterproof grease, for maximum endurance. If you have a fancy bike with fine oil instead of grease in the bearings (3 speed hubs *must* have a high-grade, fine oil like Sturmey Archer oil or ten weight Automatic Transmission Fluid), you should check and oil the bearings once every month.

Hand brakes: Keep adjusted so that the end of the lever travels about two inches when you apply the brakes fully. Check the shoes to make sure they aren't cockeyed or loose. [See chapter 2]

Changer: 3 speed. Adjust the indicator. Make sure the knurled locknut is tight against the adjusting sleeve. [See page 166]

10 speed. Check the control lever adjustable bolts. Check the range of the changer and adjust with the adjustable screws. [See pages 178, 184]

Pedal: Check to see that the spindle is locked against the crank. [See page 132]

1. Tools

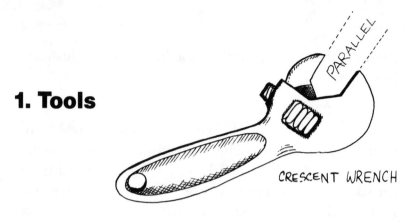

PARALLEL

CRESCENT WRENCH

● *Very necessary.* No list of tools can be absolute. There is always another tool that might be useful in a certain situation. And there is usually some way to get something done without the appropriate tool, human ingenuity being what it is. But this first list is really basic. These tools are as essential to bike repair as pedaling is to riding a bicycle. They're probably tools you have lying around the house; if not, you can buy them for less than 20 bucks.

1, 3, 10. *Crescent wrench* (adjustable end wrench). Get a good one. Attributes of a good one are: forged body, milled and hardened jaws, a precisely made adjustable jaw. To test one, open the adjustable jaw and see if you can wiggle it in such a way that it moves up and down in relation to the body of the tool. A good crescent wrench will wiggle very little, and the jaws will stay parallel. Six-inch size is best.

1, 3, 10. *Screwdriver.* One with a forged steel shank and a thin blade end is what you want. The tip should be ¼ inch wide, and the shank 4 or 5 inches long. I used to have an old Singer sewing machine screwdriver that was given away with the machine. Its handle was just a loop of the same metal as the blade. It did almost everything and was pocket-size as well. But I lost it.

3, 10. *Cable clipper.* The best is the heavy-duty bicycle cable clipper that grabs the cable in a diamond-shaped

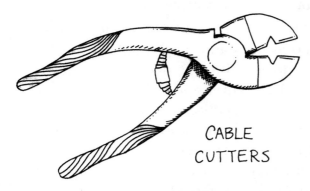

CABLE
CUTTERS

hole and shears it off clean. It'll cost you money but save you loads of time and patience. Get one from a dealer or order it from one of the bicycle catalogues. The chomping types of wire cutters (such as the ones on needlenose pliers) will do, but if they are dull or weak, they mash the ends of the cables so you have to thread the cables through their housings before cutting them.

1, 3, 10. *Hammer.* One with a flat head is best. The smaller, the less destructive, but anything lighter than 8 ounces will be too small.

3, 10. *Pliers.* The dime store variety is OK. To be used only as directed. Not a replacement for a good crescent wrench.

1, 3, 10. *Lubricants.* A light machine oil for the chain. For 3 speed hubs a fine oil, like Sturmey Archer, or Automatic Transmission oil, the pink stuff. Also, a light bicycle bearing grease, like Lubriplate or Phil Wood waterproof grease.

● *Buy as needed:* The following list of tools and accessories is useful, but I don't recommend that you rush out and buy them all just to be prepared. They are described here so that when I refer to them in the text you will know what they are. I suggest you buy these as you need them or as the fancy strikes you.

1, 3, 10. *Multiple spanner wrench.* A flat metal thing with lots of different sized and shaped holes and slots stamped in it. Try to get a Raleigh one from a Raleigh dealer, or one that has a curve and point arrangement on it similar to the *Raleigh spanner.* The curve-and-point shape (right above the word *Spanner* in the illustration) is the essential thing; if you can't find a bike spanner that has it, go to a motorcycle shop and get a shock absorber adjusting tool for Japanese motorcycles. They're cheap and they work beautifully on most bikes.

1, 3, 10. *Vise-grip.* Get one that has jaws at least 5/8 inch broad, measured side to side.

1, 3, 10. *Channel lock pliers.* Get one with jaws that can open to 2 inches or more. *Please,* don't get carried away with the destructive potential of either the vise-grip or the channel lock. Use them only as directed. If you want to destroy things, try squishing tin cans with your vise-grip or channel lock. Tin cans recycle better than squished bikes.

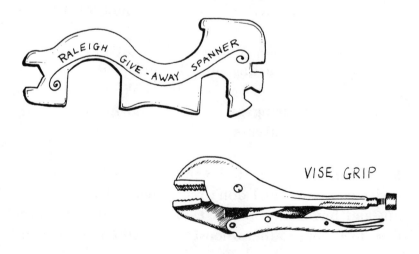

RALEIGH GIVE-AWAY SPANNER

VISE GRIP

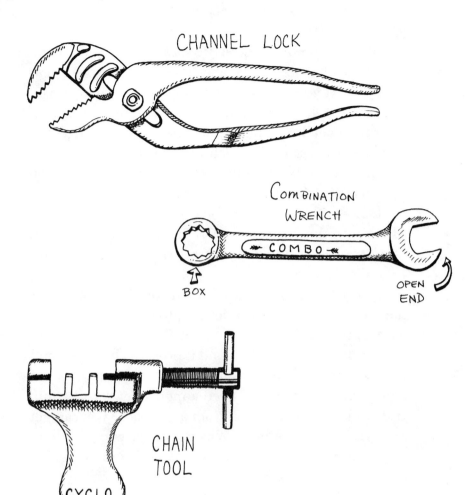

CHANNEL LOCK

COMBINATION
WRENCH

COMBO

BOX

OPEN
END

CHAIN
TOOL

CYCLO

10. *Chain tool.* For driving rivets in and out of bike chains. The inexpensive models work well and are available at most bike shops. Save the spare tip if you get one with yours, as they tend to come out of the tool and get lost. If you're plagued with tip-loss, you can blow some money on a fancy chain tool, or you can keep a close eye on the tip of your cheap one; when you see it flaring out like the butt end of a chisel where it's been hammered, just carefully file that flare off with a small metal file, so the tip won't get stuck inside the chain side-plates.

10. *Allen or hex-setscrew wrenches.* The most commonly needed sizes are 5 and 6 mm, for 10 speed gear changers. If you have a very fancy racing machine, you might need 4, 4½, 5, 6, and 7 mm Allen wrenches. If your bike needs a 6 mm Allen wrench, you can get the *Campagnolo T wrench,* which also has an 8 mm socket, for those little 8 mm nuts and bolts which abound on 10 speed bicycles. Bike shops carry these.

1, 3, 10. *Tire irons.* Not the car type. The little ones. Make sure the business end of each tool has no burrs. *Don't* try to get by with a screwdriver. Get tire irons. Bike shops have them.

1, 3, 10. *Wide-jawed wrench.* An old Ford Model A monkey wrench will do beautifully. A huge crescent wrench is best, but they cost a lot.

1, 3, 10. *Wrench set.* Box end if possible, but open end will do. If your bike is European, Japanese, or an American 10 speed, you need a metric set, 8 to 19 mm. If the bike is American and not a 10 speed, you can get an SAE 5/16 to 3/4 inch. Whichever set you get, don't expect it to have a wrench to fit every nut. When in doubt, use the trusty crescent.

1, 3, 10. *Big screwdriver.* High quality not necessary. At least a foot long.

3, 10. *Third hand.* A springy, curvy little wire thing made for holding brake shoes against the wheel. Bike shops have them.

1, 3, 10. *Metal file.* A flat or triangular one, medium size.

1, 3, 10. *Marker.* A crayon will do. A red felt pen is best.

1, 3, 10. *Magnet.* A little one, like the ones you used to play with when you were little.

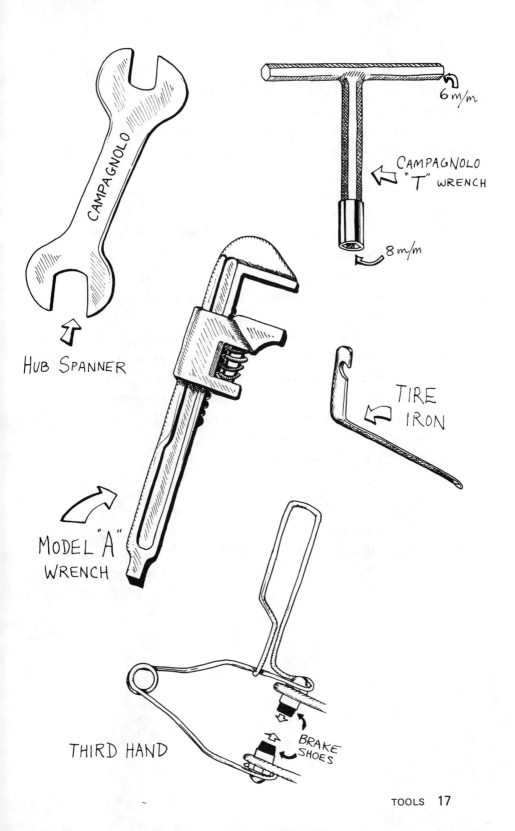

CAMPAGNOLO

6 m/m

CAMPAGNOLO
"T" WRENCH

8 m/m

HUB SPANNER

TIRE
IRON

MODEL "A"
WRENCH

THIRD HAND

BRAKE
SHOES

3, 10. *Campagnolo hub spanners.* Buy two that fit your hubs. Either a 13 and 14 mm set, or a 15 and 16 mm set. They cost a lot, but they are essential for wheel hub overhaul. Bicycle Research also makes excellent ones. Other companies make them, but most I've seen just don't last.

1, 3, 10. *Spoke wrench.* A cheap item that can get you into a lot of expensive trouble. That's why they're so cheap, and available, at any bike shop which will take on a wheel you ruin. So use *only* as directed.

10. *Freewheel remover.* A big nut with either splines or two prongs on it, depending on what kind of freewheel it fits. Look at your freewheel (the cluster of sprockets on the rear wheel of a 10 speed bike). Look at the outside end of the freewheel where it revolves around the axle. It may be hard to see in there, but look for splines or a circular ridge sticking out with two slots in it. Then see the picture of the tools and decide which remover you need. Make sure yours fits EXACTLY before you use it.

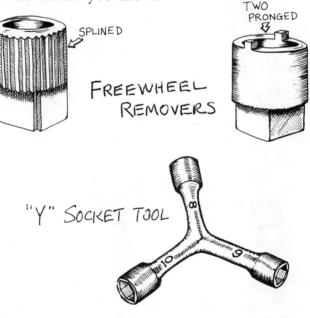

SPLINED

TWO PRONGED

FREEWHEEL REMOVERS

"Y" SOCKET TOOL

3, 10. *"Y" socket tool.* A nifty little thing that fits easily in your hand, fits all those 8, 9, and 10 mm bolts and nuts on bikes, and gives you enough leverage to tighten them, but not strip them, if you're halfway careful.

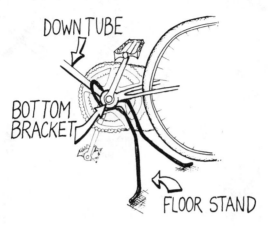

1, 3, 10. *Floor stand for bike.* You can buy a big fancy stand like they use in shops, but if you don't mind bending over or kneeling (I *like* doing homage to my bike that way!), you can use a simple rod-type stand that will hold the bike upright with the back wheel off the ground. You can get these stands from the better catalogues, or some super-nice shops with the home-repair guy in mind. In a pinch, you can use any car-rack, wall-hook, or even a fence post to get the bike up off the ground.

Catalogues for Tools and Parts:

BIG WHEEL LTD.
340 Holly Street
Denver, Colorado 80220

BIKECOLOGY
Catalogue Dept.
P.O. Box 1880
Santa Monica, Calif. 90406

CYCLOPEDIA
311 North Mitchell Street
Cadillac, Michigan 49601

SINK'S BICYCLE WORLD
816 South Washington Street
Marion, Indiana 46952

2. Brakes: General

SCUFFY SKILLMAN ONE-FOOT BRAKE
(MEMORIAL ILLUSTRATION)

(cl) means clockwise, and usually tightens a bolt or nut. (c-cl) means counterclockwise, and usually loosens a bolt or nut.

1, 3, 10. DESCRIPTION AND DIAGNOSIS:
Your bike has either hand (caliper) brakes or a foot (coaster) brake. The coaster brake only stops the rear wheel, and is not as efficient as good hand brakes, but it will work for children and for low-speed cycling for adults. Fancy disc brakes have been made for bicycles, but they are either so heavy or so expensive that they seem foolish except on a super-fancy tandem. If you have a coaster brake and have any problem with it sticking or not grabbing, the problem is a major one inside the hub of the rear wheel. You can try a little fine oil, but I do not recommend that you try over-hauling your own coaster brake hub. Turn to *Wheel Removal*, remove the rear wheel, and take it to a reliable shop for an overhaul or replacement.

3, 10. If you have hand brakes, you can do brake repairs yourself. The brake system consists of three units. There is a hand lever unit, a cable unit, and a brake mechanism unit for each wheel. [See Illustration 2] Any of the three units can develop stickiness or malfunction. If something obvious happens, like a cable gets frayed, or the mechanism is bashed all cockeyed, go to the unit involved, below. But if your brakes get the *"stickies"* (a disease almost as common to brakes as the common cold is to man), *first* find out which unit is acting up. Apply the brake. Does it stay on? That's usually the rub. Heh. Move the hand lever back to its normal position. If it moves freely, it's OK and the problem is in the other two units, cable and mechanism. If the hand lever doesn't move freely, it has the stickies. [See *Hand Lever Problems*] If the problem is in the cable or mechanism, loosen (c-cl, and you don't have to dismantle it, so just loosen) the nut on the cable anchor bolt which holds the cable at its mechanism end. Don't pull the cable out of the housing yet! Cables are hell to get back into their housings sometimes, especially if they're old and frayed. [See *Brake Cable*] Pull the anchor bolt end of the brake cable with one hand and operate the hand lever with the other. When you release the lever, does the cable fail to return to your pulling hand? If so, and the lever is OK, then

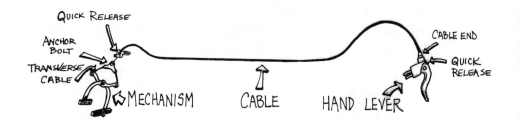

Illustration **2**   THE THREE UNITS OF A BRAKE SYSTEM

the cable must have the stickies. [See *Cable Problems*] Cable OK? That leaves the brake mechanism. Try squeezing and releasing it with your hand, fingers reaching through the spokes and pressing the shoes into the rim of the wheel. If the shoes fail to spring away from the rim, the mechanism has got the stickies. [See *Mechanism Problems*]

Hand Lever Unit

(cl) means clockwise, and usually tightens a bolt or nut. (c-cl) means counterclockwise, and usually loosens.

3, 10. DESCRIPTION: The thing you grab to put on hand brakes. The unit is attached to the bars either by two easy-to-get-at screws on the sides of the post, or by one hard-to-get-at screw down inside the post. [See Illustration 3] Many 10 speed bikes have an extension for the hand lever, a thing known as a "safety" lever, even though it is anything *but* safe in most cases. It fits on a specially long lever axle which protrudes from the hand lever post. The extension lever curves around under the horizontal central portion of a racing-type Maes handlebar. It is attached to the regular lever by means of a big screw.

10. PROBLEMS: *Stickies,* 10 speed. Let me ask, as an old-fashioned hardnose, do you have one of those "safety" lever contraptions described above? If you do and the stickies seem even remotely connected with the extension, unscrew (c-cl) the big screw that holds the extension, take the whole damn thing off and throw it away. Cut off the end of the axle that the screw went into, if you want to make your hand lever smooth like a normal one. The brake lever extension is a dangerous lazyman's item. It won't put on the brakes adequately when squeezed, unless the brake is adjusted perfectly.

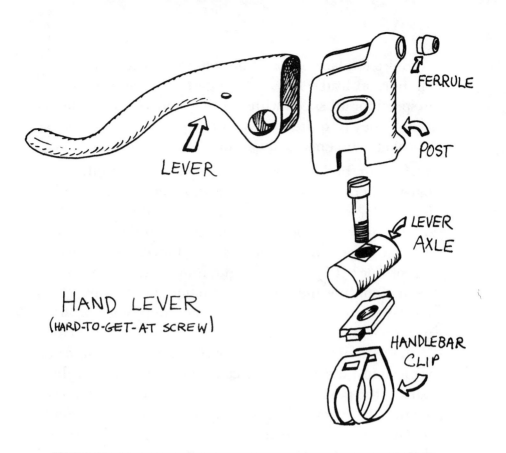

LEVER

FERRULE

POST

LEVER AXLE

HANDLEBAR CLIP

HAND LEVER
(HARD-TO-GET-AT SCREW)

HAND LEVER
(EASY SCREW)

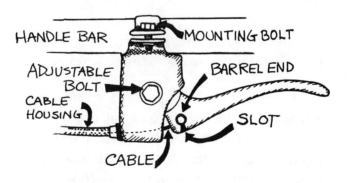

HANDLE BAR

MOUNTING BOLT

ADJUSTABLE BOLT

BARREL END

CABLE HOUSING

SLOT

CABLE

Illustration **3**   TWO DIFFERENT BRAKE HAND LEVERS

If you're too lazy or too clumsy to move your hands to the normal brake levers, I suggest you trade in your 10 speed for a 1 speed with training wheels. Or an exercycle. They're quite nice, you know, and you can put lots of attachments on them. Like brake "safety" levers.

If your brake stickies are in the lever itself, you have either an unlubricated unit, a bent lever, a bent lever axle, or a misshapen post. Try a little dab of light oil on the lever axle; that's the easiest thing. No luck? The most common problem is a bent lever. Is the lever out of line? If it is, try straightening it with your bare hands, holding the post in one hand and bending the lever with the other. If that doesn't help, you can try using various metal-eating tools, such as the vise-grip. If the axle on which the lever pivots is bent, you can replace just the axle, if you can find a shop that has the part. If the post is misshapen, so that the casing scrapes against the lever (you can observe this symptom from the underside of the lever), try sticking your screwdriver in between the post casing and the lever and twisting the screwdriver gently to free the lever. If these procedures don't solve the problem, get a new hand lever unit. [See *Slippage* below if you have trouble getting at the screw that holds the unit to the handlebars.] Don't ever bend any brake part repeatedly without replacing it. Bending fatigues metal, and you don't want your brake to break when you need it.

3. *Stickies or looseness* of 3 speed brake lever. An adjustable bolt with a locknut holds the lever in the post. [See Illustration 3] Loosen (c-cl) the nut. Loosen (c-cl) or tighten (cl) the adjustable bolt as needed. You want the bolt to be tight enough to keep the lever from rattling around, but not so tight that it gives the lever the stickies. When the adjustable bolt is adjusted cor-

rectly, tighten (c) the nut. Not too hard—they're easy to shear off.

3, 10. *Hand lever slippage.* Your hand lever unit slips on the handlebar, or you are replacing a lever. [See Illustration 3] On allrounder bars, the tightening screws are easy to get at, on a clamp around the bar. Simply tighten (cl) them.

10. On Maes bar brake levers, the screw which tightens the lever clamp on the handlebar is often down inside the lever post. To get at it, you have to release the brake cable (that means take the tension out of the cable so that the brake lever relaxes and swings freely). Whatever kind of brake you want to release, you have to grab the brake mechanism and squeeze the brake shoes against the rim. Use the third hand tool if you have one. Stick it through the spokes of the wheel and stretch the wire loops over the brake shoe nuts. On some center-pull brakes, the short transverse cable on the brake mechanism can then be released by pulling the barrel on one end of the transverse cable out of its prongs. [See Illustrations 11 and 12] With the transverse cable loose on the mechanism, you can work this looseness back up to the hand lever. On other, less convenient models, the transverse cable cannot be released, or, in the case of side-pull brakes, there is no transverse cable to release. In this case, check for a quick-release mechanism. It is right up the cable above the brake mechanism. [See Illustration 3a] It is a 1 inch lever with a round handle on it that you can pull up, away from the mechanism, to partially release the brake. Take the resulting looseness in the cable back up to the hand lever and you're ready to get at the post-tightening screw. If you have neither a quick-release gizmo nor an easily loosened transverse cable, you have an inconvenient brake system. Don't worry,

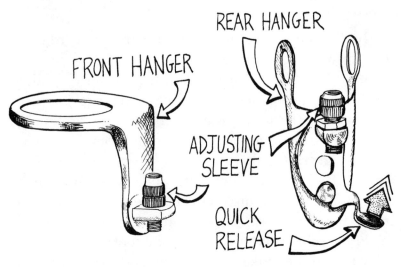

Illustration **3a** CABLE HANGERS

there's an easy solution; just loosen the cable anchor bolt that holds the end of the main brake cable at the brake mechanism. [See Illustration 7] Try to avoid pulling the end of the cable all the way out of the cable anchor bolt, especially if the end of the cable is frayed into strands. A frayed cable end is hard to get back through the little hole in the cable anchor bolt.

10. When you have loosened the brake cable by hook or by crook, pull the brake hand lever all the way down, as if you are jamming the brake on. Look down inside the hand lever post. Aha! That little screw head or hex nut down there is what you have been trying to get at. If you have the type with a screw head [see Illustration 3], you're in luck. Just wiggle a screwdriver past the cable (if the end of the cable is held in a notch, it's easy to take the cable end out of the notch and pull it out of the way) and tighten up the screw clockwise. Counterclockwise loosens the thing, but don't loosen it until it comes out. Getting it back in is a tricky operation.

If your model has a hexbolt head down there, you

need a socket to tighten that bolt. It might be an 8 mm bolt head if the bike is old or fancy. Otherwise, it is probably a 9 mm nut. Use the Campagnolo "T" wrench socket, or the proper socket on the "Y" wrench [see page 18] to tighten the bolt down in there. Don't try to use a tool that won't work, like your fingers, or a crescent wrench, or a vise-grip, or your teeth. You'll just mess up the nut. When you have tightened the nut, you have to reset the brake, by reversing whichever procedure you used to loosen the cable. A third hand is a big help. If you run into trouble, see *Cables, Brakes loose.*

Cables

(cl) means clockwise, and usually tightens a bolt or nut.
(c-cl) means counterclockwise, and usually loosens.

3, 10. DESCRIPTION: The brake cable runs from a notch or hole in the hand lever, through an end ferrule which fits or screws into the brake lever post, then through a cable housing (which is sometimes interrupted so that the cable runs bare next to a frame tube), another end ferrule, and finally, through an anchor bolt which holds the cable at its mechanism end. [See Illustration 4] The housing ferrules or "sleeves" at the ends of the cable housing are often adjustable, by being screwed in (cl) and out (c-cl), thus shortening or lengthening the distance the cable goes through housing. [See Illustration 5] The sleeve may be screwed into a quick-release lever, especially on center-pull brakes [see Illustration 3a] If you have lots of trouble with your sleeve and quick-release for your rear brake, just take the whole thing off and replace it with a TA hanger bolt, which you can get from the better shops and catalogues.

3, 10. **PROBLEMS**: *Brakes loose (adjusting the brakes).* You are screaming down the Italian Alps on your Cinelli and you see a hairpin curve coming up. Or you are cruising down to the corner market on your trusty rattle-trap and you see the grating of a gutter drain that you never noticed before, about four feet in front of your front wheel, and it looks like your wheel is going to drop between the bars. In either case, you slam on the brakes. Nothing happens for a terribly long instant. The next thing you realize is that you are watching the ground coming up at you. You should have tightened those cables, brother. It's no guarantee that you will never have an accident, but at least it will give you a fighting chance.

3, 10. The idea of *adjusting the brakes* is to give the brake cable the proper tension. It's the proper tension if the end of the brake lever travels about 2 inches when you fully apply the brakes. If the lever travels much farther than that, your brakes are too loose and you may suddenly find that they don't brake. If the end of the brake lever travels much less than 2 inches, your brakes may never completely stop braking and you know you've tightened them up too much.

To tighten a brake that's only a little loose, check to see if there is an adjusting sleeve at one end of the cable

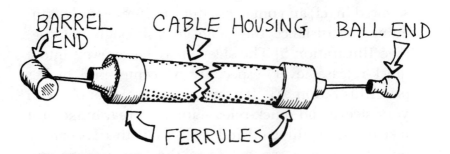

Illustration **4**   BRAKE CABLE WITH TWO DIFFERENT ENDS

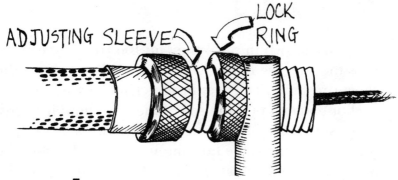

Illustration **5**   ADJUSTING SLEEVE FOR BRAKE CABLE

housing or the other. [See Illustration 5] If there is, loosen (c-cl) the lockring and screw the adjusting sleeve out *(counterclockwise)* until the cable is fairly tight. Then hand tighten the lockring (clockwise). This adjustment is sometimes easier to do if you can clamp the brake shoes against the rim while you are doing the adjusting. Use your second hand, your third hand tool, or a friend. If the sleeve comes all the way out of its threads, or even nearly all the way out, you need to take up the slack in the cable, so screw the sleeve all the way back in (clockwise) and see the next paragraph.

3, 10. *To tighten a new brake cable or one that's really loose,* first make sure the wheel is round and wobble-free so it won't rub against the tightened brakes. Pick up the bike and spin the wheel. Does the rim stay right in the middle between the brake shoes? If so, fine, go on to the brake adjustment below. If the rim wobbles, hops and blips as it passes between the brake shoes, you have to straighten it [see *Rim wobbles,* page 97]. If the wheel is cockeyed or loose so it is always too close to one brake shoe, loosen the axle nuts and align it, as on page 88.

When your wheel is straight, apply the third hand. Stick it through the spokes and stretch the two wire loops over the brake shoe nuts. Make sure the brake shoes are drawn in until they hit the rim. If the shoes miss the rim, see *Brake Shoes* below. When you get the shoes drawn in firmly against the rim, loosen the cable anchor bolt and pull the end of the cable until it's tight. Make sure the cable is seated at all points—that means the ferrules, the cable housing in the ferrules, and the blip (barrel end or ball end [see Illustration 4]) on the end of the cable in the hand lever. Everything the way it's going to stay when you panic-stop? OK. Hold the anchor bolt and pull the cable as tight as you can, then tighten up the nut on the anchor bolt. [See Illustrations 7 and 12]

10. With center-pull brakes, holding the anchor bolt up and the cable tight, while tightening the anchor bolt at the same time, is a trick that seems to require a fourth, fifth, and sixth hand. You can use a tool they call a "fourth hand" to hold the cable tight, but if you can't find or afford the tool, use one of *your* hands to hold the cable down and the carrier with the anchor bolt up. Pinch the cable between your fingers and nudge the carrier up with your knuckles; that's all the tool does. Then tighten the nut on the anchor bolt just a bit with a wrench such as the "Y" wrench. Don't try to tighten it too much or you'll just twist the bolt around and around, thus loosening the cable. Get the nut just tight enough to hold the cable still. Now let loose of the cable and the carrier with your other hand, grab a second wrench, such as a crescent, and do a two-wrench tighten of the anchor bolt and nut. Do it very thoroughly so you can actually see that the cable is squished inside the anchor bolt. But don't strain the thing so hard that you strip it. That bolt is pretty small, right? The torque, or twist, used to tighten it should be pretty small.

3, 10. Now that you have the brake cable back together again, test it. Still loose? Try the whole procedure again; it takes some practice to keep all those damn things together when you're trying to tighten the anchor bolt. If the brakes are so tight that the wheel won't go around, try applying the brakes hard. Usually the cable will stretch and the housing will shrink a little so that the wheel will free itself. If just one of the brake shoes is hitting and the other one is well off the rim, see *Brake Mechanism, One-shoe-drag.* When the whole cable setup is adjusted right, you can ride in peace. You've got a safer bike.

3, 10. *Stickies.* You have ascertained, by the diagnostic method in *Brakes: General,* that your brake cable is sticking. The problem is that the cable is binding against a ferrule or the housing somewhere. If the cable is new, try a little oil at the ends of the housing before you do anything more drastic. If the cable is old and frayed, replace it. Whenever there are cable stickies, the cable is being worn and weakened. So get a new cable, especially if yours has frayed or broken strands at any point other than the end. To remove an old cable, loosen the cable anchor bolt and pull the cable out from the hand lever end. Take the old one to a bike shop and make sure you get a new one with exactly the right shape and size end piece on the hand lever end. There are barrel ends and ball ends and mushroom ends [see Illustration 4], and all in different sizes. So take the old cable and match it, and make sure you are getting a new cable that's long enough. If the new cable seems too long, leave it that way—don't cut it down to size. If you cut it, it will be harder to get through the housing, especially if you use the mashing type clippers to cut it. You can cut it later. If you live in a wet area, or near the beach, where your cables will always get rusty and sticky, you can get fancy teflon-cased cable and housing sets; they stay slick and sticky-free longer.

Now the question is: do you have to get a new cable housing at the same time you get a new cable? You may or may not. Check all the ends of the cable housings. Are they kinked or bent at the ferrules? Especially at the hand lever? This is quite often the case. Almost as often, the problem is that the housing was cut improperly, so there is a burr on the end of the housing wire which cuts into the brake cable. In either case you can try to cut the faulty housing end off. Cut as little as possible. To make a clean housing cut, one that doesn't have a burr digging into the brake cable, take your clippers (diagonal clippers work best for this) and slowly start to squeeze in on the cable housing. Wiggle and twist as you squeeze, so that the clippers go in between the coils of the housing wire, instead of mashing a coil flat. When the clipper has worked its way slowly into a slot between the coils, squeeze harder and twist the clippers as you cut through. Check the new

RIGHT

WRONG (BURR)

Illustration **6** CABLE HOUSING CUTS

end of the cable housing for burrs. [See Illustration 6] Is there one pointing out into the air? You can clip it off with the mashing type clippers, or file it down. If there's a burr sticking into the hole in the middle of the housing, you have to make another cut. Remember to twist as you cut. It takes a little practice. But don't use a housing with a burr that's going to dig into your cable and gradually ruin it. Ever notice how you only break a shoelace when you're in a hurry? The same logic works with brake cables. When a brake cable snaps, it's usually when you really need it.

3, 10. If your old housing is really kaput, and you have to get a *new housing,* buy a big long piece of housing, with plenty of extra for mistakes, from the bike shop. On some models you will notice that to get the old housing off, you have to loosen little metal clips which attach the housing to the frame tubes. *Don't* undo those clips completely! If they just snap off and on, OK, you can undo that kind, but if they are the kind that are screwed together with a tiny screw, for the sake of your sanity, don't unscrew the little bastards all the way. Just loosen them a little and pull the housing out through them. You might want to hold the bands still while you're pulling the housing out so they won't scratch up your paint job.

When you get the old housing out, measure and cut the new pieces the same size as the old. Use the housing cutting procedure described above. Work the clippers into a slot in the housing coils, then use that little twisting motion as you cut the wire to avoid making burrs. [See Illustration 6] When the housing is cut to the right length, slide it into place and check to see if it fits into the ferrules. Is the diameter of the housing too big? If it is, you can strip ¼ to ½ inch of the cloth or plastic housing cover back and just stick the bare housing coils into the ferrule. See that the lengths of housing are just right. Put the ferrules on the ends of the housing and set the ferrules against the stops on the frame tubes.

10. If you have the kind of rear brake cable that has no housing along most of the top tube, make sure that the short piece of housing for the rear brake under the seat is the right size. If it's too short, it will break the cable. If it's too long, it will curve way out and hit your thigh muscle every time it bulges by, which can get to be a bug on a 500 mile tour.

3, 10. Before *threading a brake cable* through its housing, check the place where the cable end fits into the hand lever. Is it a cylinder thing with a hole in it? If so, start the cable threading procedure by running the whole cable through that hole before you thread it through the housing. If there is a little slot, thread the cable into the housing first, then insert the cable end into the slot. To thread the new cable through new or old housing, hold the housing out straight, put a little grease or oil on the cable, and run it through, twisting it slightly as you go. Twisting clockwise? Twisting counterclockwise? Glad you asked. The idea of twisting is to keep the cable from unraveling, right? You want to twist the cable the opposite way from the way it's wound, so that the ends don't catch and come undone. Just look at the cable and see which way it twists, and think about which way you will have to twist it into the housing in order to keep the cable from untwisting. Get the idea? Good—go ahead and do it. When the cable is all housed, check it for stickies. Hold the mechanism end of the cable in one hand and pull the hand lever with the other. Sure hope it's smooth. If not, find where the problem is and cut that section of housing over.

Don't cut the cable down to size before you have put it through the hole in the anchor bolt. Tighten up your brand new nifty brake cable according to the procedure in *Cable Problems, tighten a new brake cable.* Leave about 2 inches of cable sticking out past the anchor bolt, and clip off the extra. Ride in peace. You have a good, safe brake cable.

Brake Mechanism: General

(cl) means clockwise, and usually tightens a bolt or nut.
(c-cl) means counterclockwise, and usually loosens.

3, 10. The brake mechanism is the thing that puts friction on your wheel to stop you; when you squeeze the hand lever, the brake shoes on the mechanism should squeeze the rim of the wheel. When you release the lever, the brake mechanism should completely release the wheel. There are two distinct types of hand brakes: side-pull and center-pull.

Side-Pull Mechanism

(cl) means clockwise, and usually tightens a bolt or nut.
(c-cl) means counterclockwise, and usually loosens.

3, 10. DESCRIPTION: The kind with the cable anchored on one side of the mechanism. The cable housing is stopped on one of the brake arms, and the cable itself is anchored on the other. [See Illustration 7] The mechanism is attached to the bike frame by a pivot bolt. The pivot bolt, you will find, if you take it out, holds together a zillion indescribable parts. And the thing won't work correctly unless you get them all together exactly right. So let's get them straight. [See Illustration 8] Starting at the end of the pivot bolt which is farthest from the frame, there is first an acorn

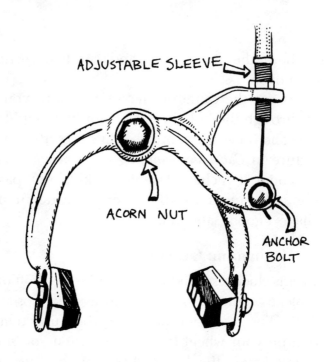

ADJUSTABLE SLEEVE

ACORN NUT

ANCHOR BOLT

Illustration **7** SIDE PULL BRAKE

locknut, then an adjusting nut, then a washer (often a wide one with writing on it), then the longer of the two brake arms (known as the outer arm), then a thin washer, then the branched brake arm (the inner arm), then a third washer (often a thick one), then a seating pad (which is fixed on the bolt, or screwed on tightly; it has a slot in it which holds the brake spring either above or below the pivot bolt). Then the pivot bolt passes right through the frame, through another seating pad (shaped to grab the round frame tube), a lock washer of some sort, and finally a tightening acorn nut.

3, 10. What's that you say? You don't have all those parts on yours? You might have the kind of pivot bolt with a screw-head instead of the acorn nut and locknut. Other than that, you are missing some parts.

On the lower end of each of the brake arms is a bolted-on brake shoe. Somewhere above the brake shoe on each arm is a small pole sticking out which holds an end of the brake spring. The spring, usually a surprisingly powerful bugger, loops from one of the brake arms above or below the pivot bolt to the other brake arm.

PROBLEMS: *One-shoe drag.* One of the brake shoes refuses to come off the rim of your wheel when you release the brakes. First, check to see whether the whole brake mechanism is loose on its pivot bolt. If it's loose, so that the whole thing waggles back and forth and the tightening nut [see Illustration 8] turns freely, just

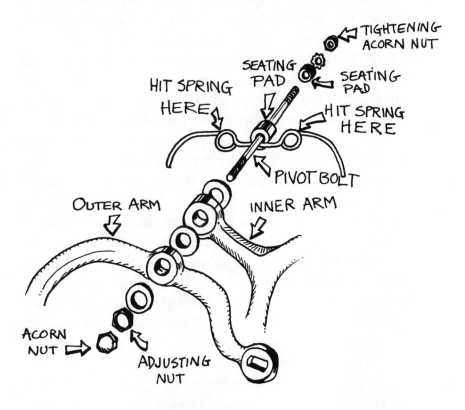

Illustration **8**   SIDE PULL MECHANISM: EXPLODED VIEW

tighten that nut up (cl) while holding the mechanism by the arms so that the shoes are both clear of the rim. If the tightening nut isn't loose, try loosening it (c-cl), then moving the mechanism by the arms to the right position, and tightening the nut again (cl), making sure to hold the arms in the right position as you tighten the nut. One brake shoe still insists on coming in on the rim? Take a good look at the shape of the seating pad which is against the frame tube on the mechanism side. [See Illustration 8] This might be the same part that holds the brake spring. If it isn't, you should be able to get that shoe off the rim by using the above procedure. But if it is, the arms are going to come back to the same incorrect position no matter how many times you loosen the tightening nut. You have to bend the spring to move the pushed-in shoe off the rim. First tighten up (cl) the tightening nut. Take your hammer, your big screwdriver, and your knowledge of these tools' destructive tendencies, and approach the brake spring from above. [See Illustration 8] Set the tip of your big screwdriver on the topmost point in the curve or loop of the brake spring on the side *where the shoe is off the rim.* Got that? The opposite side from where the shoe is rubbing. Set the screwdriver as near as possible to vertical (the handlebars or the seat may make it a little awkward; the longer the screwdriver, the better) and give the screwdriver handle a tap with the hammer, lightly. No luck? Shoe still on the rim? Be firmer. But go easy. It's all too easy to bend the spring too far, or put a big nick in it, or the frame tube, or your hand. Apply and release the brakes to check your shoe position when you think it's right.

3, 10. *Stickies.* Neither brake shoe will come off the wheel when the brakes are released. You have come here from *Brakes: General, Diagnosis,* or you have eliminated the possibility of stickies in the cable and hand lever units. First, check the nuts on the ends of the pivot bolt, especially the acorn nut and the adjusting nut next to it on the mechanism end of the pivot bolt. [See Illustration 8] These two nuts should be locked against each other, and *not* locked against the brake arms. If the nuts are locked against the brake arms so that the arms can't budge, first make sure that the tightening acorn nut is tightened up (cl) well. Then loosen (c-cl) the acorn locknut, then the inner adjusting nut. The inner nut must be tightened up (cl) against the brake arm, then backed off (c-cl) ½ turn. Hold the adjusting nut still with a thin wrench if you have one, or a pair of needlenose pliers. When you have a good hold on the inner nut, tighten (cl) the locking acorn nut firmly against it (not so hard that you strip the threads). The inner nut must not move while you are doing this. Still have a sticky mechanism? Try a little oil on the pivot bolt. Work the mechanism by hand, and let the thing sit a while, to get the oil worked in. Be patient. Go away, give your bike seat a little saddlesoaping, or go say hello to a friend or a spouse who thinks you spend too much of your time tinkering with your bike.

3, 10. When you think the oil has sunk in, work the mechanism by hand some more. Smoother? Or still got the stickies? The trouble might be that the brake arms are rubbing together. First make sure there is a thin washer between the two arms. If not, that's the problem. If there is one, then probably one of the arms is bent. Check near the branched end of the inner arm (the shorter one) to see if it is rubbing the other arm. To separate binding brake arms, stick a medium-size screwdriver between them and twist firmly. They will usually spread apart easily, then spring back when the screwdriver is removed. So twist several times on the screwdriver, but go easy. If the brake mechanism is still sticky, something very basic is wrong with it and you should take it apart completely.

To begin the *overhaul*, remove the nuts on both ends, undo the spring (careful—they bite), then release the cable anchor bolt, and slowly take everything off the pivot bolt. Remember the order of the parts. [See Illustration 8] The pivot bolt or the arms may be bent, or one of the many parts may be missing. Try straightening or replacing any parts that look like they need it. Compare the parts with ones on a mechanism like yours that works. Consider buying a new mechanism. Getting parts for brake mechanisms is not easy. And most new mechanisms are cheap. If you have taken your old mechanism apart, review the order of things on the pivot bolt before you try to put the mechanism back together. When the arms and washers and nuts are on the pivot bolt, tighten (cl) the adjusting nut against the arms, then back it off (c-cl) ½ turn and lock the acorn nut against it, holding the adjusting nut in place with a thin wrench or needlenose pliers. Set the spring before you attach the mechanism to the frame of the bike. Setting the spring usually involves some awkward squeezing and pushing, and the spring often jumps out and tries to nip your knuckles. Set one end of the spring into the arm that has the branch (the inner arm), then get a good grip on the other end of the spring with the dimestore variety pliers. Grab with the very tips of the plier jaws, either at the end of the spring or up from where it will catch on the brake arm. Keep a tight grip on the pliers as you set the spring. That spring wants to get loose and take a nip at you, remember. When resetting the brake, do the cable-anchoring procedure (squeezing the brakes together with the third hand, then slipping the cable through the anchor bolt, then tightening up the anchor bolt [see *Cables*]). Release the third hand before you tighten the tightening acorn nut on the pivot bolt. When tightening up that nut, try to see that neither brake shoe is hitting the rim. If one is when you finish, see *One-shoe drag* above. If both shoes are rubbing, see the section on adjusting the cable.

The ultra-light side pull

Center-Pull Mechanism

(cl) means clockwise, and usually tightens a bolt or nut. (c-cl) means counterclockwise, and usually loosens.

10. DESCRIPTION: The kind which has the cable anchored to a carrier that pulls on a short transverse cable, which in turn pulls the brake arms. [See Illustration 9] There are two pivot bolts and two springs. The pivot bolts of the center-pull mechanism pass through a washer, the brake arm, and a spring, and are mounted on the bridge. The bridge is held by a long bolt to the bike frame. [See Illustration 10] On the long bolt, between the bridge and the frame, there is sometimes a washer and always a seating pad which conforms to the curve of the frame tube. On the opposite end of the long bolt from the mechanism there is a smaller seating pad, a washer, and finally a tightening acorn nut.

10. PROBLEMS: *One-shoe drag.* When the brake is released, one of the brake shoes does not come off the rim of the wheel, and the other shoe goes way off the rim. The whole mechanism is cockeyed. The idea is to straighten it by rotating the whole business around the long bolt until the shoes are centered around the rim. It will rotate more easily if you loosen the tightening acorn nut on the end of the long bolt (just loosen it— don't take it off). Then grab the brake arms with your hands and rotate your mechanism. The bridge should shift slightly on the seating pad. Get each of the shoes the same distance from the rim. Then tighten up (cl) the acorn nut. If, in pulling on the arms, you pulled the brake shoes out of place, see *Brake Shoes,* below.

Stickies. The brake shoes do not release the rim of the wheel when you release the hand lever, and you have checked the cable and lever for stickies. The prob-

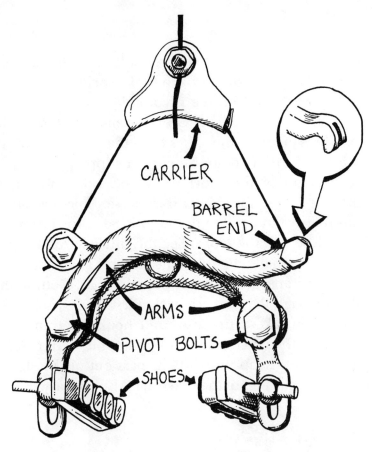

CARRIER

BARREL END

ARMS

PIVOT BOLTS

SHOES

Illustration **9**   CENTER-PULL BRAKE MECHANISM

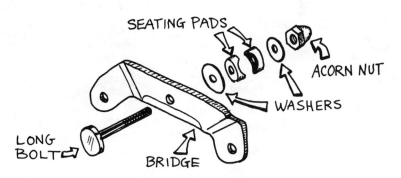

SEATING PADS

ACORN NUT

WASHERS

LONG BOLT

BRIDGE

Illustration **10** CENTER-PULL MOUNTING BRIDGE, EXPLODED VIEW

lem is either unlubricated pivot bolts, bent brake arms rubbing together, or a broken brake spring.

Try a little oil on the pivot bolts. To work the oil in, first *release the brakes.* On some models this can be done by squeezing the shoes onto the rim by hand, or with the third hand, and then just slipping the barrel on one end of the short transverse cable out of its curved prongs. Your short transverse cable has barrel ends that are trapped in two loops? [See Illustration 11] Look closely at the loops. See the little slot on the top of the loop that's closest to the frame? That slot is for the short transverse cable to pass through. Getting the cable through that slot is a trick. First apply your third hand, then take a tire iron and hook the transverse cable with the notch in it. With that cable well hooked, you can pull it up until it will pass out of the slot in the loop at the end of the brake arm. But go easy. If you

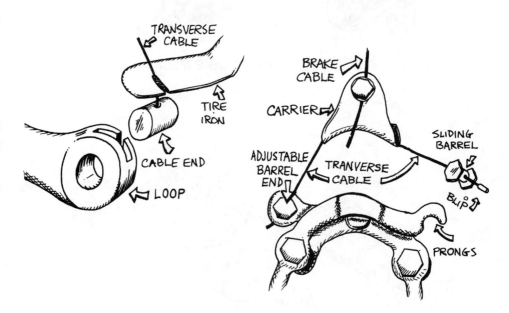

Illustration **11** TRANSVERSE CABLE RELEASE
WITH PRONGS AND LOOPS

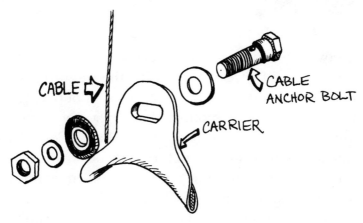

Illustration **12** TRANSVERSE CABLE CARRIER,
EXPLODED VIEW

pull too hard on the short transverse cable, you'll kink it. So if you can't get it, loosen (c-cl) the cable anchor bolt that's attached to the long cable that goes to the brake handle, then take the short transverse cable out of its slot with ease. One note here. If you have the kind of carrier with the short transverse cable held in a lip of metal, the main cable should come down on the *opposite* side of the carrier from this lip. [See Illustration 12] It's more convenient there. If your main cable comes down on the same side of the carrier as the lip, so it fouls you up when you're trying to get the transverse cable out, you can correct the problem by undoing the main cable anchor bolt and reversing it in the carrier. Now put your main cable back in where it belongs.

When the short transverse cable is released, try working the brake arms in and out by hand. Still sticky? You oiled in vain? Check to see if the arms are bent and jamming against each other. On most models, the arms should not touch each other at all; the two surfaces should be flat and clear of each other. If they aren't, pry them gently with a screwdriver. Some have a tiny red-plastic-covered bump sliding in a little groove down in between the arms. If it's jammed, work the arms and spread them with the screwdriver until the bump is loose again. If it takes a lot of prying to get the arms free of each other, they must have been given quite a bash to get so bent out of shape. Consider getting a new mechanism. Bending metal weakens it, and rebending it to get it straight weakens it again. Don't tempt brake breakage.

If you're going to get a new mechanism, you'll have to take off the old one. Take off the transverse cable as described above, then remove the tightening acorn nut that's on the long bolt. Take your old mechanism to a bike shop and get an exact replacement. When you put on a new mechanism, make sure you have all the seating pads and washers in the right order on the long bolt. [See Illustration 10] Set the brake shoes straight and tighten up the nuts that hold them. [See *Brake Shoes*] Then set the mechanism so that each of the shoes is the same distance from the rim and tighten the acorn nut up on the end of the long bolt. To set the cable on your nice new mechanism, see *Cables, tighten a new cable*.

Center-pull overhaul. If you find that your brake arms aren't rubbing, your stickies might be due to a broken spring or a bent pivot bolt, and replacing one of them involves a pretty basic overhaul. *Warning:* Individual replacement parts for brake mechanisms are hard to find. You will probably have to buy a whole new brake mechanism in any event, so maybe you don't want to bother with the overhaul. On the other hand, if you can get the individual parts, or if you think the problem might be just crud in the works, or if you're miles from anywhere with no other choice, or if it's a rainy afternoon at home and you've got nothing else you'd rather do, then this overhaul is for you.

Start the *overhaul* by releasing the transverse cable as described in *Stickies* above. Next release the springs. If the end of a spring which is stopped on the brake arm extends beyond the little pole which holds the spring end, get your screwdriver and stick the tip between the spring end of the brake arm, and twist and pry that spring loose. Careful—keep fingers out of the way. Brake springs bite. When you have the springs loose, unscrew the pivot bolts (c-cl). Make sure you're using a wrench that fits. Those pivot bolts have thin heads and they get messed up easily. When you have taken a pivot bolt all the way out, one of two things will happen, depending on what kind of brake you have. Either the bolt will come out and the brake arm will stay on a pole that's attached to the bridge, or the whole brake arm will come off with the bolt and a nut will fall down from behind the bridge. The first type I will call the bolt-into-pole type pivot bolt. The second type will be referred to as the bolt-and-nut type.

On the bolt-into-pole type, see if the brake arm can rotate freely on the pole. If not, take it off, watching the order of washers (if there are any), and the arm, and the spring at the bottom. Look at the surface of the pole on which the arm is supposed to rotate. Scarred, mangled, or otherwise deformed? If so, you can try cleaning it off with steel wool and a rag, or even filing it a little, but not much. If it's really pretty bad, there's nothing to do but replace the whole bridge. Brake bridges are hard to come by, so you'll probably have to get a whole new brake mechanism. If the surface of the pole is just dry and a little dirty, clean it up and clean the inside of the sleeve through the arm which turns on the pole. Then put a drop of oil on the pole and replace everything, spring first (make sure it's stuck in its hole or slot in the bridge), then a washer (if your model has one), then the arm, then another washer (if you have one), and finally the pivot bolt. Now you have to set that nasty spring. Watch it! It wants to bite your fingers. Try laying your screwdriver shank along the back of the brake shoe, and shoehorning the spring with the screwdriver blade to catch it behind the post. OW! Gotcha, didn't it? Well, call it what it is, and try again. When you get the thing back together, reset the transverse cable (for help see *Broken transverse cable*). Check the brake shoes. You may have twisted them. [See *Brake Shoes, Cockeyed*]

If you have the bolt-and-nut type pivot bolt, first pick up that nut I told you fell out from behind the bridge. If it didn't fall out or if it's in *front* of the bridge (as on some models), screwed onto the bolt, take it off and put it with the spring in a jar. Now take the brake arm in one hand and try twisting the pivot bolt with the other. No go? The arm is stuck to the sleeve that goes through it. Carefully notice and remember what goes where on the pivot bolt as you take things off. Pull off the plain washer that's tight around the pivot bolt (if there is one on your model). The next thing around the bolt is a beveled washer. Pull the bolt out of the arm and this washer will fall off. Is this or the beveled washer on the other side of the arm messed up? You should be able to get a replacement. If you can't, you have to replace the whole mechanism. Take the old one with you and match it. There are several different sizes and differences between front and rear, so get the same one. Hopefully you can replace the beveled washer, or you can manage to clean up the washers and the sleeve that goes through the brake arm (if you have one) enough that the arm will turn freely on the pivot bolt. If your pivot bolt is bent you can try to straighten it with the vise-grip, but that is a stopgap measure at best. Bent pivot bolts should be replaced. Oil the pivot bolt lightly, put the washers, the sleeve (if you have one), the arm, and the spring (make sure it's right side up) back on the bolt in the right order, and then tighten the pivot bolt into the nut that fits behind the bridge. If your model has the nut in front of the bridge, spin the nut (cl) onto the bolt until it is tight against the beveled washer. Then back the nut off ½ turn (c-cl), and screw the bolt into the threaded hole in the bridge (cl). As you tighten the bolt, make sure the nut stays where you just put it and doesn't back into the brake arm. Whichever kind you have, screw that bolt up good and tight, but not so tight that you shear it off or mangle the bolt head. Check for free rotation. If the arm is restricted, loosen the pivot bolt and make sure something isn't squished against the brake arm where it shouldn't be, like a beveled washer or (if you have it) the nut in front of the bridge. When you have the arm working, you have to reset the spring. Remember that the spring would love to bite your finger. Try putting your screwdriver shank along the back of the brake shoe and shoehorning the spring onto its pole. You might twist the brake shoes cockeyed while working on the spring; if so, see *Brake Shoes, Cockeyed.* Reset the transverse cable as in *Broken transverse cable,* below, and you're set to go.

Broken transverse cable. If the short cable that crosses from one brake arm to the other is broken or frayed, you've got to replace it. There are two different types (as with everything else about brake mechanisms). One type has fixed barrels on the ends, and the other type has one barrel end that slides on the cable until it hits a blip at the end, and another barrel that can be adjusted by screwing it up tight like an anchor bolt. [See Illustration 11]

With the fixed-barrel type, *replacement* is simple. Apply the third hand to the brake shoes. Stick one barrel in the end of one of the brake arms, then thread the cable through the carrier (you may have to loosen the anchor bolt if your carrier is a box with metal sides). When the short transverse cable is hooked at one end and through the carrier, take the loose end of the cable and press the barrel into the loop at the end of the brake arm. You can't get that cable through the slot on the brake arm? Hold the barrel part way into the loop, take a tire iron, and hook the transverse cable with the notch in the iron. [See Illustration 11] Draw up on the transverse cable until it will go through the slot in the loop at the end of the brake arm. If the thing is still too tight, don't try so hard that you kink the transverse cable. Just loosen the cable anchor bolt on the carrier, loosen the main cable, then slide the short transverse cable into its slot with ease. To tighten up the main cable properly, see *Cables, Tightening a new cable.*

To replace the kind of short transverse cable with an adjustable barrel at one end and a sliding barrel at the other end, put the adjustable barrel (without the cable) in place in its arm. [See Illustration 11] Thread the free end of the transverse cable first through the sliding barrel end, and then through the adjustable barrel end so that the cable is 1 to 2 inches longer than the distance between the ends of the brake arms. Anchor the end of the transverse cable by tightening (cl) the adjustable barrel end. Once anchored, this kind of transverse cable is easy to attach. Just slip the transverse cable into the carrier and pop the barrel end into its prongs on the brake arm. Now you probably will have to adjust the main brake cable, so turn to *Cables, Tightening a new cable.*

Brake Shoes

(cl) means clockwise, and usually tightens a bolt or nut. (c-cl) means counterclockwise, and usually loosens.

3, 10. DESCRIPTION AND DIAGNOSIS: There are two types of brake shoes. The most common type is mounted by bolts to the brake arms on all side-pull brakes and some center-pull brakes (that's the *plain type* in Illustration 13). On other center-pull brakes, the shoe is attached to a smooth pole, which is in turn clamped tight to the brake arm by an eyebolt (the *eyebolt type* in Illustration 13). All this means is that the eyebolt type can pivot as well as slide up and down. This makes it a little harder to be sure that the brake shoe stays straight as you tighten up on the nut that holds it, but there's a good reason for the complication. The eyebolt allows you to change the angle at which the brake shoe hits the rim. Some rim walls flare out more than others. You can set the eyebolt brake so that

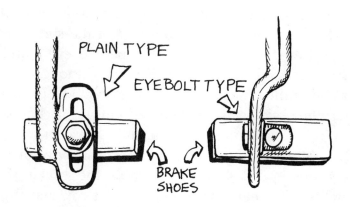

Illustration **13** BRAKE SHOES – TWO DIFFERENT TYPES

it not only hits the rim, but hits it flush, no matter what angle the rim wall is at. This will give you excellent braking power.

3, 10. PROBLEMS: *Brake shoes cockeyed.* The brake shoes are not grabbing the rim correctly, because they are too high or too low, or because they are slanted and not parallel to the rim. Brake shoes are pretty simple. [See Illustrations 9 and 13] They are held to the brake arms by a bolt and a nut (or an eyebolt and a nut). Loosen (c-cl) the nut, and you can set the shoe by hand so that it will hit the rim correctly. Make sure that the shoe is both parallel to the rim *and* at the right level so that it grabs the rim when you apply the brakes and not the tire above or nothing below. If the brake shoe goes into the tire, it tends to wear the tire out. Fast. ZZZZZ BAM! Like that. When you get the shoe where it should be, hold it there while you tighten up the nut (cl). Careful. Those bolts strip easily. Now check it to make sure the shoe didn't move while you were tightening.

3, 10. *Brake shoe toe-in.* Your brake shoe might be cockeyed, not up and down, but in and out, so that one end of the shoe toes in and hits the rim way before the other. Don't worry if the front end of the shoe hits a little before the rear end; some people even prefer their shoes toed in that way. Do worry though if the rear end of the brake shoe is hitting first. The problem is that the brake arm or a shoe is bent. Replace a bent shoe. To straighten a bent arm, use a crescent wrench with care. Apply it to the arm either just above or just below the brake shoe (don't grab the brake shoe assembly with that wrench—it will destroy that thing before you can blink). Turn it gently until the shoe is at the proper angle. It doesn't take much to get it right.

And it doesn't take much more to twist the thing right off. If that happens you'll have to get a whole new mechanism, as replacement arms are very difficult to come by.

3, 10 *Worn brake shoes.* Your brake shoes are worn down to the metal, or hardened with old age. *Warning:* If your brakes make you feel insecure, don't just replace the brake shoes and go on your way, hoping for the best. If something about the brakes is spooky, chances are changing the shoes won't solve much. Check the rest of the brake system. The actual process of changing the brake shoes is simple. Before you take the shoes off, though, take a look at them a minute. Notice how the front end of each brake shoe is closed off by a metal wall so that the rubber pad won't shoot out that end when you apply the brakes. Unscrew (c-cl) the nut that holds the brake shoe, remove the shoe, and take it with you to get replacements. Replace the whole shoe, bolt and all. You have to get the same type (plain or eyebolt [see Illustration 13] that your old ones were, because the new ones will have to fit the old arms. If you have trouble getting adequate braking power, especially in wet weather, you can get special brake shoes with an "X" pattern of bumps, or you can blow a big wad of money and get super-fancy Mathauser brake shoes, which have cooling fins, super-duper abrasive rubber, and optimum shape. Wow. In wet weather, you can make normal brakes work OK if you apply the brakes lightly *before* you need to stop; this whisks off the water so the brake can grip. Notice how the rubber on your old shoes is worn at a certain angle. If you have the plain type brake shoes, you should try to find replacements that have rubber pads with a similar angle. Or if you have the eyebolt type brake shoes, you adjust the brake shoes to fit the rim as you install them. Make sure you put them on with the metal stops in front of the rubber pads.

3, 10. *Brake shoes squeaking.* When you apply the brakes, your whole bike vibrates, and, if you are going fast, your brakes screech like a Model T Ford with its original brake shoes. My own brakes often sound like this, and I don't let it bother me too much, as long as the brakes still do their job. But if the sound bothers you, first check the rims of the wheels. Are there streaks on the rims where some of your brake shoe rubber has worn off onto the metal and stuck there? That might be it. Clean the rims with Ajax or some other cleanser (nothing so strong that it will damage the smooth surface of the rim, like steel wool) and look for uneven places on the rims. It doesn't take much to make a brake shoe start rubbing off on a rim. You might need a new rim. *See Spokes and Rims.* The next thing is to adjust the toe-in. [See *Brake shoe toe-in*] It may stop your squeaking to bend the brake arms slightly with a crescent wrench (easy—remember, they break easily) so that the front ends of the shoes hit a little before the rear ends. But don't get carried away. The whole length of the shoe should hit the rim if the brakes are put on hard. If your brakes still screech, don't fret, as long as they work.

If the brakes "judder" so the whole bike shakes, this may be due to a loose long bolt or pivot bolt (the bolt that holds the mechanism to the frame). Tighten the bolt and see if the mechanism still chatters away against the frame when you apply the brakes. If it does, it may be bent, or you may just have to put a bigger washer and/or seating pad between the mechanism and the bike frame [see Illustrations 8 and 10].

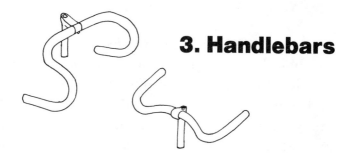

3. Handlebars

(cl) means clockwise, and usually tightens a bolt or nut. (c-cl) means counterclockwise, and usually loosens.

1, 3, 10. DESCRIPTION: Handlebars, made of steel or aluminum, come in many different shapes. The Maes-type and the allrounder-type are the most common. [See Illustration 14] The Maes bars can be put in a wide variety of positions. I haven't seen any yet with the ends pointing straight up in the air, but I expect to. Most people who have to ride any distance put their Maes bars in such a position that the ends angle down at the ground towards the back of the bicycle. This will usually make the top of the bars horizontal through the first ninety-degree bend. Many reputable riders tip the Maes bars forward somewhat from this position. The faddish, upside-down position of the Maes bars is unsafe. It invites impalement. You like it? You can have it. Speaking of impalement, handlebars must *always* have something over or in their open ends. I don't care if it's a super-adjustable neoprene plug, or a plastic grip, or an old champagne cork; just keep something stuck in the ends of your handlebars. I literally owe my life to the fact that I've always had my bars plugged.

The handlebars are held to the stem by a keyed or fixed binderbolt and a nut. [See Illustration 17] Allrounder bars usually have grips, and Maes bars are usually wrapped with cloth or plastic tape to improve the rider's grasp.

1, 3, 10. PROBLEMS: *Bars loose in stem.* That means the handlebars slip around, but the stem does not. Position the bars as described above, or to your taste, and tighten up (cl) the nut on the binderbolt. If tightening up the binderbolt nut just spins the binderbolt around, the key or "dog" that's supposed to hold the binderbolt still has been sheared off. Loosen (c-cl) the nut, holding the bolt head with a vise-grip if necessary. Take the sheared-off bolt to a shop and get an exact replacement. If the slot in the handlebar for the key has been ruined, get the kind of binderbolt that has a hex head on it so you can hold it with a wrench. Reassemble [see Illustration 17].

1, 3, 10. Whether using a standard or hex head binderbolt, make sure you get the nut very tight. First put a drop of oil on the threads of the bolt so the nut will cinch up smoothly. Check the fit of your wrench (a box end wrench is best, and a carefully used crescent is better than a loose open end wrench), then really tighten up. Test for slippage by pushing and pulling on the bars.

1, 3, 10. If your handlebars slip because they are obviously too small in diameter for your stem, you can

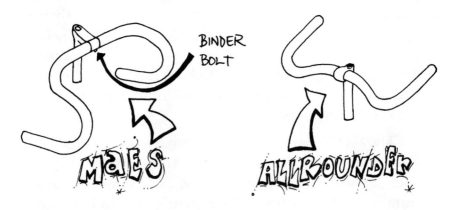

Illustration **14** HANDLEBARS

Illustration **15**
STRAIGHTENING
A BENT
MAES BAR

get a shim (sometimes called a ferrule), a thin, curved strip of metal which fits between the bars and the stem, so that the stem can be bound up snug on the bars.

1, 3, 10. *Handlebars too high or low.* To raise or lower the handlebars, you have to loosen and tap on the expander bolt (the one in the stem) so the stem can slide up and down. When the bars are the right height, tighten (cl) the expander bolt again. Always leave at least 2½ inches of the stem inside the headset; on many stems there is a line marking this limit.

10. *Maes bar bent in.* You've taken a spill, right? You are scraped and shook up, but OK. The bike is OK too, except that one of the handlebars has a new bend in it, so that it toes in. When you stop shaking, put the bike on its side so that the still-straight bar is flat on the ground. Step on the drop portion of the straight bar (careful, don't break the brake lever) and pull firmly upward on the folded bar. [See Illustration 15] If the bars are aluminum, you might be able to get them straight enough to ride. Steel bars are a lot harder to

bend. And any bar that has been bent and unbent is weak, so when you get a chance, get a replacement.

1, 3, 10. *To replace handlebars*, first get the grip, tape, brake lever, horn, or whatever off the old ones. Then loosen the binderbolt completely. Slide the bars out and take them to a shop. Get ones that are the same diameter at the stem or a little smaller. If you get smaller ones, get a shim so the new bars will fit the stem. Don't get bars that are too big for your stem— they will stretch and weaken the stem.

10. *Tape worn or unwound.* Take the plugs out of the ends of the bars. If there is a screw in the middle of the plug, unscrew (c-cl) it until it is loose, then push it in and work the plug out. If your plugs don't have screws, just yank them out. Unwind the old tape completely. Get new tape. I recommend either cloth or the rubbery, stretchy type of plastic tape which is thicker in the middle than at the edges. You can use the extra-thick tape, or you can put on several layers of standard tape for a softer feel on your bars, but it can get to the point where you are out of touch with that zingy responsiveness of your bike's front end. Start wrapping the tape about 3 inches out from the midpoint of the bar where it is held by the stem. [See Illustration 16] If the tape

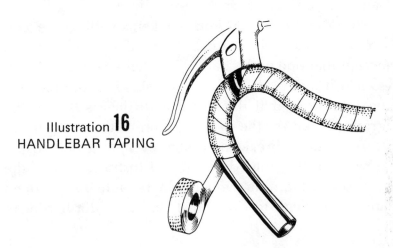

Illustration **16**
HANDLEBAR TAPING

has no gum on it, you can stick the end down with a little piece of Scotch tape. Whichever type of tape you use, start by wrapping a couple turns in one place to cover the tape end. As you lay the tape on, keep it tight, and make it go directly from the roll to the bar. There's less to get tangled up that way. Overlap at least a third at all points. At the bends, you have to overlap more on the inside then on the outside. Just make sure it overlaps enough on the outside of the bend. Angle the tape across the bar behind the hand lever, making sure it is tight all the time. [See Illustration 16] At the end of the bar, leave a little tape to tuck in under the plug. (By the way, you can tuck things in there if you're travelling or crossing borders, although I've heard that

STEM
(GOOSENECK)

4. Stem

(cl) means clockwise, and usually tightens a bolt or nut.
(c-cl) means counterclockwise, and usually loosens.

1, 3, 10. DESCRIPTION AND DIAGNOSIS:
The stem, or gooseneck, as it is often more descriptively
called, is a curved or angled piece of tube, one end of
which holds the handlebars, the other end of which fits
inside the headset. The stem holds the bars in a binding
clamp which is either welded to the bars or, more often,
tightened onto the bars by means of a short binderbolt
and nut. [See Illustration 17] The end of the stem which
sticks down into the head tube of the frame rotates
freely, turning the front wheel back and forth, because
it is not attached to the frame tube directly but to the
tube which comes up from the fork. [See Illustration
21] The bottom of the stem is wedged inside that fork
tube by means of a long expander bolt which literally
expands the diameter of the bottom of the stem until it
is jammed tight against the surrounding fork tube.

10. Some of you 10 speed bike owners might wonder
why your handlebars are so low. You might be tempted
to raise the stem up. Don't. The top of the stem should
be slightly lower than the top of the seat. (If the seat is
sticking way up in the air, the problem is not the stem,
but that the frame is too small.) Do you find the bent-
over riding position uncomfortable? Go buy a little
sting-ray type bike and wear your tail out. The low
position of the bars and the shortness of the stem on
serious bicycles keep you bent over so you don't destroy

your sitzplatz. OK? Just try riding an hour or so on a bike that keeps you sitting upright, and you'll see what I mean. The bent-over riding position also increases your pedaling power and decreases your wind resistance. The Wright brothers, who knew a lot about wind resistance, invented the bent-over riding position. There *can* be problems with stem extension, however. You may find that, as you ride, either your knees are almost hitting the handlebars, or you have to stretch out so far to reach the bars that your arms and back ache all the time. First make sure you have the right frame size and seat position [see *Frame* and *Seat* chapters].

If your frame is the right size, you might have the wrong length extension on your stem. The extension is the length of the horizontal part of the stem. [See Illustration 17] There is no rigid formula for stem extension. The formulas I have seen are absurdly complicated. (If you decide to get a new stem with a different extension, see *Stem replacement* below.) Find a stem you can live with, and get accustomed to it. Ride more and worry less about the stem extension—that's my advice.

1, 3, 10. PROBLEMS: *Your stem is loose,* so that your handlebars turn independently of your front wheel. Or your *stem is crooked.* You crooked stem people may be riding straight down the road, but your handlebars are aiming off to one side. Or your handlebars are aiming straight down the road, but your bike just insists on going into the ditch. You've got to straighten up and tighten up. Go around to the front of the bike and hold the wheel between your legs. (Don't get kinky with it—just hold it.) Grasp the handlebars firmly with both hands and straighten them so that the stem extension lines up with the front wheel. (What's

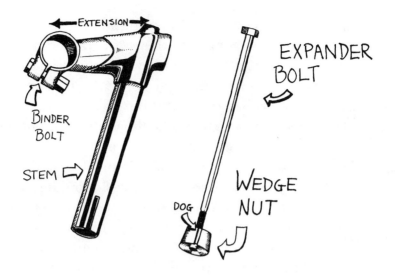

Illustration **17** STEM OR "GOOSENECK"

that? You can't straighten the bars? Loosen the expander bolt [see Illustration 17] two full turns. Then tap down on its head with a hammer so that the stem comes unwedged. Now straighten the handlebars.) Tighten up on the long expander bolt. An expander bolt should be tight enough to hold the stem, but not too tight. Try twisting the bars again. If they don't slip unless you pull quite hard, then the expander bolt is tight enough. The expander bolt should not be so tight that the stem can't slip if you crash. If you fall on the bars, you want *them* to give, not you. So don't tighten up on the expander bolt too much.

If tightening the expander bolt has no effect, the wedge nut at the bottom of the bolt is disengaged from the stem. [See Illustration 17] Pull up on the expander bolt. If it doesn't come all the way out of the stem, pull it as far as you can, then tighten (cl) it by hand while pulling upward until the head of the bolt is snug. That solves your problem, so now you can return to the paragraph above and finish tightening the expander bolt with a wrench. If when you pulled up on the expander bolt it came all the way out on the stem, then the wedge nut has fallen off. In that case, twist and pull the handlebars and stem all the way out, then turn the bike upside down and shake the wedge nut out. Put the expander bolt back in the stem and screw on (cl) the wedge nut [see Illustration 17] until that little ridge (dog, they call it) just fits into the slot on the stem. Now you're ready to attach the whole business to your head-set, so turn to the second half of *replacement* below.

You have a little *crack* in your stem. *Don't* ride with a cracked stem, especially if yours is an alloy one. Replace it! Now! No kidding—it's a terrible way to crash, having your stem break off.

To replace a stem, or to install a different stem if you have been referred here from above, you have to take the tape and brake lever off one end of the handlebar (see *Brake Hand Lever Slippage* if your lever is hard to get off), then loosen (c-cl) the short binderbolt [see Illustration 17] and slide the handlebar out of the stem. To release the expander bolt, unscrew (c-cl) it about two full turns, so that the head of the bolt rises up off the stem. Then take a hammer in one hand, hold onto the stem firmly with the other hand, and lightly tap the head of the expander downward with the hammer. It shouldn't take much to get the stem loose. Take it to the shop and match a new one. Also get a roll of handlebar tape. Most stems are nearly the same diameter where they fit into the fork tube, but there are a number of different handlebar diameters. If you have to get a stem with a handlebar clamp that's too big for your bars, you can get a little sleeve of metal, called a shim (or sometimes a ferrule) that will fill the gap.

But if your bars are too big to fit in your new stem, change the stem. Don't stretch the clamp on the stem. It might break. When your bars are back in the stem [see *Handlebars*], push *at least* 2½ inches of the stem down into the headset. If the stem fits so snugly into the tube down inside the headset that you can't push it down, loosen the big locknut that's on top of the headset [see Illustration 18]. This will let the tube loose a tiny bit, so the stem will slip down in. Now you need to straighten and tighten your stem, so turn to that section above. Then replace the brake lever [see *Brake Hand Lever*] and put on new handlebar tape [see *Handlebars*].

5. Headset

HEAD TUBE

(cl) means clockwise, and usually tightens a nut or bolt. (c-cl) means counterclockwise, and usually loosens.

1, 3, 10. DESCRIPTION: The headset holds the front fork of the bike to the frontmost, or "head," tube of the frame. [See Illustration 19] A long tube comes up from the fork through the frame and is held in the headset bearings. The top of the fork tube comes right up to the top of the head tube, so that you can stick the stem down into it and steer. There are a lot of parts around that fork tube. [See Illustration 18] Starting right at the crown of the fork [see Illustration 19], there is the fork crown bearing race, then the bearings, then the bottom set race, then the head tube, then the top set race, then the top threaded race (removable by un-screwing), then a washer (sometimes threaded and screwed up tight against the threaded race), then the cable hanger (sometimes omitted—if there is one, it will probably have a little flat or "dog" that fits into a corresponding shape on the fork tube), and finally, on top, a big locknut.

PROBLEMS: *Headset loose.* The front of the bicycle clanks when you go over bumps. If you get off the bike and lift the front wheel off the ground and drop it, there is a clank. The fork seems loose in relation to the rest of the frame. Any of these very common symp-toms tell you the same thing. Either your front wheel is loose, or your headset is loose. Check the wheel to

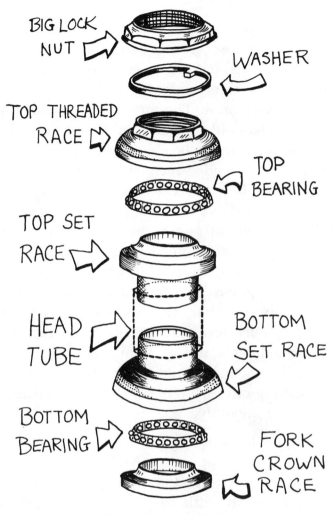

BIG LOCK NUT ⇨

WASHER ⇦

TOP THREADED RACE ⇨

TOP BEARING ⇦

TOP SET RACE ⇨

HEAD TUBE ⇨

BOTTOM SET RACE ⇦

BOTTOM BEARING ⇨

FORK CROWN RACE ⇦

Illustration **18** HEADSET, EXPLODED VIEW

make sure. Let the bike sit normally on the ground and see if you can wiggle the front wheel back and forth with your fingers, either on its bearings or in the fork. If the wheel is loose, see *Hubs.* If the front wheel is solid, that clanking you've noticed is due to a loose headset. There are very few headsets that will stay tight forever, so you should get used to tightening yours every year or so.

To tighten your headset, first loosen the locknut, which is the topmost big nut of the headset. [See Illustration 18] Tighten (cl) the threaded top bearing race, which is the next thing under the locknut that has some gripping surface on it. The threaded race might have flat outer surfaces like a nut, or a cross-hatch pattern that you're supposed to be able to grip with your bare hands. If your threaded race has flat surfaces so that it looks like a big nut, you're in luck. Use a huge crescent wrench if you have one, or the Ford monkey wrench if you can find one, or the channel lock wrench, or a vise-grip or even a pipe wrench if you don't mind chewing the thing up a bit. Jiggle and turn the handlebars as you tighten the threaded race, to make sure everything is seated in the headset. You shouldn't have to put much torque (twist) on the threaded race because you don't want it so tight that it squeezes the bearings. The idea is to tighten the bearings enough so that nothing rattles, but not so tight that the headset doesn't rotate smoothly.

Test for rattles by lifting the front wheel 2 inches off the ground and dropping it. If you have to turn the threaded race around and around before you can get rid of the clank, the little ball bearings have probably fallen out, due to excessive headset looseness. Naughty you! You should have done this adjustment *long* ago. Turn to the *overhaul* procedure two pages below, and rebuild your headset with new ball bearings.

When you have the adjustment just right, bring the washer and cable hanger (if you have one) back down on top of the threaded race. If your model has a threaded washer, that washer now has to be locked against the threaded race. This kind of threaded washer has notches in it. Use a curve and hook spanner [see *Tools*] or set a screwdriver into a notch, aiming clockwise, so that you can tap the screwdriver and drive the lockwasher down tight. Do it gently. Your bearings are at stake. Screw the big top locknut down (cl) until it is snug. Try tightening down on it, using a spanner, like the Raleigh give-away if you can get one, or a big crescent, or the Ford monkey wrench, or, if you can't do better, the channel lock wrench.

If tightening the big top locknut tightens the threaded bearing race at all, *stop tightening.* Your bearings are at stake. If the threaded bearing race is getting tight, hold onto the top locknut with one wrench, and back (c-cl) the threaded race off the bearings with a second wrench. This tightens the threaded race up against the top locknut, which is what you want. The two-wrench method is the best, if you can get two wrenches that big. You can use the vise-grip on the threaded race, if you don't clamp down too hard, but don't use a vise-grip on the top locknut—it is too easy to squish out of shape. If you have a lot of trouble with the tools you can get hold of, don't knock yourself out or mash up the threaded race or the big top locknut in the process. Take the bike to a good shop. They will have the right tools to do the job.

Headset stiff, or sticky. You find it difficult to steer your bicycle, or, when you steer, ugly cracking or grinding noises come out of the headset. Or when you are riding down a bumpy hill and put on your brakes, all kinds of cracking noises come from the headset. For any of these symptoms, first determine where the problem actually is. Take the front wheel off the bike [see *Wheel Removal*]. To make sure that the wheel isn't actually the trouble, hold the ends of the axle in your hands and spin the wheel. Does the axle tug and jerk in your hands or slip back and forth in the hub? If so, you have wheel hub trouble. If the wheel glides evenly on its axle, you can assume the trouble is in the headset. Just to make sure, check the stem where it fits down in the headset. Are there a good 2½ inches of the stem sticking down into the fork tube? If the stem wiggles at all when you push it back and forth, go to the *Stem* chapter and see if you can't take care of your noisy front end with some stem tightening. It isn't the stem? The problem must be the headset.

The headset might need adjusting and lubrication. The bearings might be dirty and worn. The races might be misshapen, or, worse, the frame might be misshapen in such a way that the races don't mount parallel to each other. Start with lubrication and adjustment. Follow the procedure for a loose headset, then lay the bike on its side and drip some oil down into the bearings. Does that help? No? Ah, well, can't win 'em all. If your headset needs more than oil and adjusting, it needs a complete overhaul. So have at it.

Start the *overhaul* by laying the bike down on its left side with a clean white rag under the headset (bearings are easier to find on white rags). Loosen (c-cl) the expander bolt that's on top of the stem two full turns, then tap the bolt head with a hammer to unwedge the stem inside the fork tube. Twist and pull the handlebars to get the stem out. Remove the front wheel if you haven't already. Now you can start dismantling the headset. [See Illustration 18] Use a big wrench to take the big top locknut off and put it in a can or jar where you won't lose it. Take the washer off and put it in the same place, and the cable hanger if you have one. Before you take the top threaded bearing race off, think a minute. That threaded race is the only thing

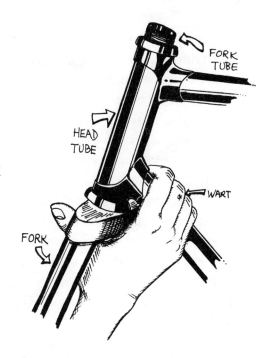

Illustration **19**
HOLDING FORK
IN HEADSET

FORK
TUBE

HEAD
TUBE

WART

FORK

left holding the fork tube in the frame. When you undo it, the fork tube will want to slip and flop around, sending ball bearings all over the place. So, to keep things simple, leave the bike lying on its side, and hold the fork up against the frame with one hand while you loosen the top threaded race with the other hand.

As the top threaded race spins its way up the fork tube, you will begin to see one of three things. Either a number of big ball bearings will start falling out from under the top threaded race, or another inset race will appear with tiny bearings falling out of it, or you will see ball bearings held in a retainer, a neat little metal ring that fits around them. Everybody, take the top threaded race all the way off the fork tube, still holding the fork in place in the frame with one hand. Get all the ball bearings out of the top threaded race and the top set race. If they aren't in a race, count them. How many are there? Write that down, here   so you won't forget. There are so many different kinds of headsets, all with different numbers of bearings, that I can't tell you how many bearings your headset should have. Collect all the bearings and put them in your jar with the other headset parts. If your headset is the kind with the tiny bearings and the inset race, take the inset race off and put it into the jar too.

Make sure the fork crown end of the headset is over the white rag, and draw the fork out. Bearings will come raining down on the rag. Count them. Get any that are stuck with grease to the race or the fork tube or the frame or your nose, and put all the bearings in the jar. (If you have an inset bearing race, put it in the jar too.)

Take the fork crown bearing race (the bottom-most one) off the fork tube. If it is stuck to the fork, take a screwdriver and gently pry it free, working your way around and around it, prying just a little at a time. You don't want to bend or scar that thing. When you get it off, hold it a second and look at it. If you have the inset bearing races with the tiny bearings, you will notice that the fork crown race is very similar to the inset races. Can you see the difference? That's right. The inset races have curved outer surfaces, and the fork crown race has a flat outer surface. Now that you know and see the difference, you can put both races together in the container.

Whether or not you have the inset bearing races, you will have two large races that are set (hence the name *set* races) into the frame of the bike. Look at them. If they sit flush against the frame all the way around, leave them alone. If not, they may be bent or the frame may be bent. The races are easier to replace than the frame, so hope it's the races. To take bent races out,

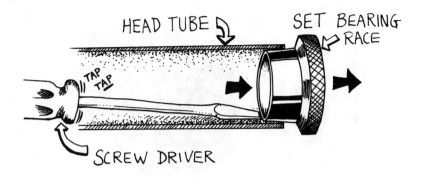

Illustration **20** TAPPING OUT A SET RACE

twist them back and forth with your hands. If they turn, take them out with your hands. If they are too tight to get out with your hands, stick a foot-long piece of pipe or the big screwdriver down the frame tube. With the bike still on its side, put one end of the pipe or screwdriver into the frame tube and slide it all the way in until it stops against the lip of the bearing race at the other end. Lift the end of the pipe that's sticking out of the frame tube, so the pipe goes through the frame tube diagonally. Get a friend to hold the frame while you gently tap the pipe with a small hammer. (A friend is an incredibly useful aid which I failed to mention in the tool section. Get one at least.) Work around and around the race, gently tapping as you go. When it pops out, take it to your favorite bike shop for replacement.

If your set races are not bent, clean them with solvent. If you're not in a hurry, put some solvent in the container with all the other headset parts, and go do something for a while, like take a walk with your friend. If you're rushed, take a rag with some solvent on it and wipe off all the parts, especially the bearings and races. When all of the bearing surfaces are really

Illustration **20a**

THE PITS

PITS

SHINY RING

clean, take a good look at them. You might even use a magnifying glass. Are the balls dent-free? Is the shiny place in the race where the balls were running smooth, and the same color all the way around? Is that shiny place round? Put the races down on a flat surface, like a formica table. Do they sit perfectly flat? If the answer to any of these questions is no, buy new parts. If you aren't sure, take them to someone who knows the difference between good bearings and shot bearings. Take the old bearings to the store and match them to get *exact* replacements. (Fancy-type headsets are often too thick for the short fork tubes on standard bikes.) Get a fork, too, if needed. Whatever replacing you do, get a few extra ball bearings for spares. If you get a new headset, make sure that the threads and the lockwasher are the same as your old one and that the whole set is the correct size.

You can start *reassembly* when you have clean and/or new headset parts. Remember, frame lying on its side, clean white rag under the head tube. Clean out the head tube, then put the two set races (top and bottom) into it (unless you never took them out). The one with the bigger cup cover is the bottom one. Put a block of wood on each race and tap it home with a hammer if it's a little tight. Check all around the races and make sure they are flush against the frame. When they are, slip the fork crown race down over the fork tube till it's down flush on the crown. [See Illustration 18] That may take a little hammer-and-block treatment, but be very careful, as that little race can bend easily. Tap gently, round and round the race. Fill the grooves of both set races with grease. (If you have the tiny bearings and insets, fill both insets with grease.) Stick the ball bearings in the grease of the bottom set race (or inset) only. Remember how many there's supposed to be? If not, look back a couple pages to where you wrote it down.

If your ball bearings are in a retainer, you don't have to count them and stick them carefully in the grease. You lucky dog. Just make sure the retainer goes in right, so the solid outer ring does *not* rub against the race.

When the bearings are all in, wipe off extra grease. You don't want extra grease slopping out of the works because it attracts sand and grit, the arch-enemies of bearings. Clean off the fork and hold it in one hand. Hold the frame still with the other. Carefully guide the fork tube up through the head tube of the frame. (If you have the insets, take one of them and slip the fork tube through it until the inset rests on the crown race, then slip the fork into the head tube.)

When the fork tube is up snug, rotate it back and forth, holding it firmly in place. Roll easily? It better. If not, take it apart and have another look at things. If it feels nice (good bearings *do* feel nice—it's worth the work), hold the fork up in the frame with one hand, and with the other stick the bearings in the grease in the top set race. Does it seem ridiculous doing this one-handed? Well, persevere. Or get a friend to hold the fork in. But don't let that fork loose. With all the ball bearings in place—and still holding the fork— screw (cl) on the top threaded race. Start it very carefully on the threads at the top of the fork tube. A lot of threads get ruined at this point, and if it should happen to you, you'll have to take the fork out, take it to a good bike shop and get it threaded, then go through the whole ball bearing procedure again. So start that threaded bearing race carefully. Screw it all the way down (cl) just snug against the bearings. Now you can stop holding the fork still. Try twisting it back and forth. It should be smooth, even if the threaded race is down pretty tight. If it's tight in places and loose in others, something is wrong. Check the set races and the crown race to make sure they are flush against the frame or fork. You might have bent frame or fork problems, in which case you should turn to those chapters. You may just want to live with it, but try to remember that it's not a good idea to run into curbs. If everything looks and feels good, turn back to *tighten your headset* to adjust the bearings and finish up by replacing the wheel and resetting the brakes.

6. Fork

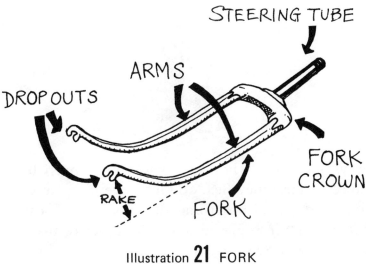

ILLUSTRATION: STEERING TUBE, ARMS, DROP OUTS, RAKE, FORK, FORK CROWN

Illustration **21** FORK

1, 3, 10. DESCRIPTION: The thing that holds your front wheel to the rest of the bike. Starting at the top, the fork has a long tube which can't be seen from the outside because it is inside the headset and the head tube of the bike frame. At the lower end of the long fork tube is a visible fork crown, into which two blades or "arms" are brazed. [See Illustration 21] On some models, the crown and the two blades of the fork are all one piece of solid metal. At the ends of the fork blades, there are little upside-down U-shaped ends, called drop-outs, because that's where the wheel drops out. Just hope the wheel doesn't until you want it to. The wheel axle fits into the drop-outs and should be held firmly there.

Forks are important. So when you get a bike, get one with good, tubular forks. The solid ones are stronger, but they are so rigid that if you hit a curb hard, or go into a drain culvert, your whole bike frame is likely to self-destruct. And the impact delivered to you will be pretty destructive too. Not that tubular forks will

always save you. They just give you a much better chance because they flex. You hit something, and they do a good job of absorbing the shock. They can be straightened or replaced a lot more easily than the frame, or you. OK? Tubular forks come with a great variety of crowns, and a great variety of bends (also called deflections or rakes). The variations affect the stiffness of the forks. The stronger the crown, and the straighter, or steeper the fork arm (i.e., the less deflection), the stiffer the fork. Stiff forks hold the road best and waste less of the rider's energy through flexing. Flexible forks give a more comfortable ride, and some people like the springy feeling they give. Take your pick. Racers take stiff forks. Touring people usually prefer more flexible ones.

PROBLEMS: *Fork bent.* Don't try to straighten it yourself! You might wind up with a dangerously mis-shapen fork. Take the whole bike to a reliable shop and ask if the fork is worth trying to straighten. They should have nifty tools and much know-how that can straighten minor bends. Replace a fork that is bent so much that the front wheel hits the frame, or any fork on which the paint just below the crown bubbled and cracked. New forks don't cost so much that you should take the risk of using a bent and rebent one. Metal that has been bent and rebent is weak—fatigued. It might give up on you when you need it most. Imagine your-self going very fast with, and then without, a front wheel. Got the picture?

To remove and replace a fork, follow the *Headset Overhaul* procedure. Check the headset while you're at it. Make sure the fork tube on your new fork is the same length as your old one. Take the old fork to the shop and have them match it.

7. Wheels: General

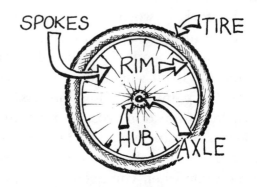

(cl) means clockwise, and usually tightens a nut or bolt. (c-cl) means counterclockwise, and usually loosens.

1, 3, 10. DESCRIPTION AND DIAGNOSIS: The round things. Each has an axle, a hub with bearings, spokes, spoke nipples, a rim, a rim strip, a tire, and a tube. (If you have sew-up tires, the tire and the tube are one unit.) The wheel is attached to the fork either by two big nuts (sometimes wing nuts) on the axle or a quick-release lever, a handy gadget, which should always be on the left side of the bike, and locked firmly in such a position that the end of the lever points diagonally up and to the rear of the bike. On the rear wheel of a 10 speed, there is a cluster of sprockets on the right side of the hub. On 3 speed bikes the rear wheel has a cable and chain (called the indicator) going into one end of the axle. [See Illustration 34] On 1 speed bikes there is a metal bracket that drops down and forward from the left side of the rear axle and clamps onto the frame (that's your coaster brake).

What you have to do most often to wheels is take them off and put them on—to do all kinds of things. [See *Wheel Removal* and *Wheel Replacement* in this chapter]

If your wheel is loose (the rear one rubs the frame if it is loose), or it doesn't spin smoothly and/or makes nasty noises, see *Hubs* in this chapter.

If your rim wobbles side to side while you slowly revolve the wheel (or you notice it while you're riding), see *Spokes and Rims* in this chapter.

Wheel Removal

(cl) means clockwise, and usually tightens a nut or bolt. (c-cl) means counterclockwise, and usually loosens.

1, 3, 10. First you have to get the wheels off the ground while you work on them. That will keep the bike from falling on its tender parts when you pull a wheel out from underneath it. It's a good idea to hang it up somehow; from an auto carrier rack, hooks, a rope over a tree limb, or just a plain floor stand [see *Tools*]. If all else fails, have your neighborhood Atlas hold it up. The more firmly the bike is held, the better. If you can't hang the bike up, lay it gently on its left side, and on some surface that won't scratch it up. Or if you have a 1 speed without any tender levers on the handlebars (and do this *only* to a 1 speed), you can stand the bike upside down on its handlebars and seat. Just remember that in the directions, "down" means down the way the bike normally rides, so for you upside-down people, "down" means up. Perfectly clear. OK, now you've got the bike in position.

3, 10. If you are removing a rear wheel from a 10 speed, shift into the highest gear to move the chain into the smallest rear sprocket on the gear cluster. If you are removing a 3 speed rear wheel, put it in high gear and find the little chain and pole that come out of the right side of the rear hub [called the indicator—see Illustration 34]. Loosen (cl) the little knurled locknut on the indicator pole, and unscrew completely (c-cl) the sleeve that's attached to the cable that goes to the hand lever. Take that loose cable end and stick it somewhere out of the way.

1. If you are going to remove a 1 speed rear wheel, you have to undo the coaster brake bracket from the bike frame. The bracket is a metal arm at the left end of the rear axle. Unscrew (c-cl) the bolt and nut which hold the bracket to a clamp around the frame tube. When the bracket is loose from the clamp, put the bolt back into its hole and screw (cl) the nut onto it, so they won't get lost.

3, 10. If the wheel has hand brakes, you might have to release them. Look down on the brake shoes from straight above. If they are far enough away from the rim that the tire will fit between them, or if you have a pump handy and can let the air out of the tire and pump it back up when you have finished replacing the wheel, *don't touch the brakes.* If it even looks like the wheel can squeeze out through the brakes, skip ahead to "ready to take the wheel off," because you are. But if you are going to have lots of trouble getting the rim or the tire past the brake shoes, you have to release the brakes.

10. For the release of *center-pull brakes,* you may have a handy quick-release lever, either right above the brake on the cable hanger, or at the top of the brake lever. [See Illustration 2] With either of these quick-release mechanisms, you can loosen the tension of the brake cable enough that the wheel will come out easily. If you don't have a quick-release lever, you will have to release the short transverse cable (the one that goes between the arms of the brake mechanism. [See Illustration 11] The barrels on the ends of the short transverse cable fit into prongs or loops on the brake arms. If you squeeze the brake shoes against the rim

with a third hand tool, or even with your own second hand, you can simply pull one of the barrel ends of the transverse cable out of its prong or loop, and the brake will be released. (If you need help on brake releasing, see the *Brakes* chapter, *Center-Pull Mechanism.*)

3, 10. Releasing *side-pull brakes* may be easier at the brake hand lever end of the system [see Illustration 2], especially if the bike is a 3 speed. Apply the third hand tool to your brake shoes, or just have a friend grab the brake shoes and squeeze them against the rim. The cable will now be loose. Push the looseness in the cable backwards through the housing to the brake hand lever. At the lever, pull the cable housing away from the brake lever post and see if there is a slot that will allow you to pull the cable down out of the post. [See Illustration 3] If there is no such slot in the lever trunk, there should be one where the cable end is attached to the hand lever. If nothing else works, loosen the cable anchor bolt at the brake mechanism [see Illustration 7], but don't let the cable slip all the way out of the anchor bolt if you can help it.

1, 3, 10. You are now *ready to release the wheel.* See what's holding the wheel axle to the frame. If there are big nuts or wing nuts around the axle, loosen the nut at each end of the axle (c-cl). It is best if you use two wrenches, or both hands if you have wing nuts, so that you are loosening at both ends at once. Remember that when you turn the nuts on both ends of the axle counterclockwise, you will be turning them opposite directions. What? How can that be? It's because each nut, being on an opposite end, has an opposite perspective. It's like the writing on your T-shirt looks funny in the mirror. Anyway, take my word for it; the nuts *do* unscrew in opposite directions.

10. If your wheel is held not by nuts but by a lever on one end of the axle and a smooth, cone-shaped nut on the other end, you have a *quick-release* device. It is a wonderful gizmo. To free the wheel, all you have to do is pull the lever loose.

1, 3, 10. Now everybody is ready to remove the wheel. If it's a front wheel, they come out so easily that it has probably already dropped out of the slots (drop-outs) in the frame that held it. If not, just pull diagonally down and forward. Rear wheels also have to be pulled down and forward out of the drop-outs, but the chain will complicate things a little. With 1 and 3 speed bikes, go ahead and pull the wheel out of the frame, and then just lift the chain off the sprocket by hand if you need to. On a 10 speed bike, first make sure the chain is on the smallest sprocket. Then stand at the rear of the bike and push the rear wheel down and forward with your left hand while you pull the derailleur (changer) back with your right hand. The small sprocket should then slip by the changer, and you can free the sprocket from the chain by hand if you need to. Don't force things. Let them come easily. If the changer falls off the bike at this point, the drop-out bolt is loose or missing. [See Illustrations 49, 50, 52] Tighten (cl) or replace it.

Wheel Replacement

(cl) means clockwise, and usually tightens a nut or bolt. (c-cl) means counterclockwise, and usually loosens.

If you have gotten your wheel off already, I assume you know what kind of device holds it to the drop-outs. Whatever kind of wheel it is, remember that any washers usually go *outside* the drop-outs.

10. If you are putting in a 10 speed *back wheel with*

a quick-release lever, loosen (c-cl) the lever a few turns, holding the cone end in one hand, and the lever in the other. Put the right gear control lever all the way forward (the way it is when you're in high gear). Now work your wheel into the drop-outs, slipping the chain over the smallest sprocket on the sprocket cluster. Set the quick-release lever so it is open (pointing straight out) and tighten up (cl) the quick-release device until both the cone and the lever ends are finger-tight against the frame. Pull the wheel toward the rear of the bike until the right end of the axle seats against a block in the drop-out. Keep the right end of the axle seated, and move the left side of the axle until the rim of the wheel is centered between the chain stays. Hold the wheel in place with one hand, and lock the quick-release lever closed. It should be pretty hard to push that lever all the way closed. If it isn't, unlock the lever, then hold the cone in one hand, and with the other hand tighten the lever about ½ turn. Align the wheel, and lock the lever closed again. Hard to lock this time? Good. Reset your brakes if they were released, and your wheel is ready for action.

10. If you are putting in a *front wheel with quick-release,* make sure the lever is unlocked (pointing straight out), and slip the axle into the drop-outs. Seat the axle in the drop-outs, then tighten up (cl) and lock the quick-release lever. Check the wheel alignment to make sure the rim is centered between the fork blades.

1, 3, 10. To replace a *rear wheel with bolt-on axle or wing nuts,* first spin (c-cl) the nuts out to the ends of the axle. If you have a 3 speed or a 10 speed, put your gear control lever in high gear.

1, 3. One and 3 speed people—put the chain on the sprocket, then work the axle into the drop-outs. You have to pull the wheel back until the chain has only

½ inch of up and down play, *and* at the same time you have to center (align) the rim of the wheel between the chain stays. With both of these conditions met, hold the wheel in exactly that position while you tighten (cl) the nuts against the frame. This could require a friend. Especially if the axle turns while you're tightening one nut, in which case you'll have to tighten both nuts at the same time. When you've got them fairly tight, and the chain slack and alignment both look good, 3 speed people start threading (cl) the indicator sleeve onto the indicator [see Illustration 34]. Make sure the control lever is in the high gear position, then screw (cl) the sleeve down until the cable has almost no slack. Lock up (c-cl) the lockring. Test the gears. Problems? [See *Power Train, Hub Changer*]

10. Ten speed people, work your wheel axle into the drop-outs, slipping the chain over the smallest sprocket. Seat both axles all the way into the ends of the drop-out slots and hand tighten (cl) the nuts. Keeping the right end of the axle firmly seated, slide the left end slightly forward until the front of the wheel is centered (aligned) between the two chain stays. With the wheel in exactly this position, tighten (cl) the nuts up well against the frame.

1, 3, 10. Whichever kind of rear wheel you have replaced, tighten up the brakes (1 speed people, re-attach the brake arm to the frame).

To replace a *front wheel with a bolt-on axle or wing nuts,* spin (c-cl) the nuts until they're near the ends of the axle, then work the axle all the way into the drop-outs. Tighten (cl) both nuts with your fingers, then make sure both ends of the wheel axle are still seated all the way against the tops of the drop-out slots. Check the alignment by seeing if the rim of the wheel is equidistant from each of the fork blades. If it's way off center, like rubbing against one of the fork blades, your forks are badly bent out of alignment [see *Forks*]. Now tighten (cl) the axle nuts well with a wrench. If tightening one nut turns the whole axle, use a wrench on each nut. Recheck the alignment, reset your brakes if they were released, and you are set to go.

Hubs

(cl) means clockwise, and usually tightens a nut or bolt. (c-cl) means counterclockwise, and usually loosens.

1, 3, 10. DESCRIPTION: A hub consists of an axle, two bearing sets, and a casing [see Illustration 22]. If you can find no evidence of bearing sets on your hub, you have one with sealed bearings; you'll never have to adjust or oil it, you lucky stiff (there are superfancy Avocet adjustable sealed bearing hubs, but even these hardly ever need care). Each bearing set has a locknut, a washer that is kept from turning by a pin that fits into a groove in the axle, a cone, the ball bearings, and a bearing cup which is pressed perma-

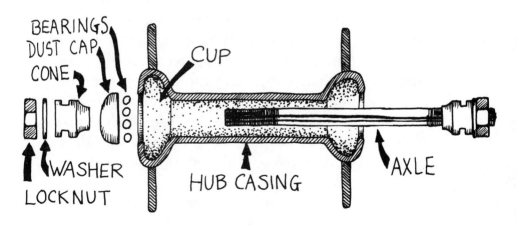

Illustration **22**   HUB, EXPLODED VIEW

nently into the hub casing. On some models there are no washers and locknuts. These models use the drop-outs (those slots in the frame) of the bike frame as a washer, and the big nut that holds the axle to the bike frame as a locknut.

1, 3, 10. PROBLEMS: *Loose wheel.* Your wheel wiggles from side to side, or rubs the frame. Fix it now. Your bearings are at stake. First, see if the wheel is loose in the frame. If it is, you just need to tighten up your axle nuts, or wing nuts, or quick-release levers, whichever you have. [See *Wheel Replacement* above] When the big nuts are tight, grab the tire and see if you can still wiggle the wheel from side to side.

If the wheel still wiggles, your problem is *loose cones.* Look at the left side of your hub. Starting at the left end of any axle, you should have first a big nut (sometimes a wing nut), then the drop-outs (the slot in the frame that holds the wheel), then a thin locknut, then a washer, then the cylindrical cone that disappears into the hub and has two slots at its outside edge for a thin spanner. Your wheel may have no thin locknut. In that case, the big axle nut acts as a locknut. Think of it as such in this whole section, and do your adjust-ment with the wheel *on* the bike. You *must* have a spanner that fits in the slots in the cones to work on your hub. Campagnolo makes a good set, if you can get them. But don't monkey with your hub unless you have a thin spanner to fit it. Your hub may have a slotted cone on only one end of the axle. If so, don't monkey with the end that has no slot in its cone (the slotted cone should be on the left side, but this isn't always the case). Loosen (c-cl) only the left big axle nut. If you have quick-release hubs, you have no choice. You pull the lever, both sides come loose, and the wheel falls out. But for *bolt-on axle people,* tightening the cones should be done with the wheel held in place by the right big axle nut.

Get your thin spanner in the slots on the left cone, tighten (cl) the cone up on the bearings, back it off (c-cl) about ½ turn, until the wheel spins easily. Then tighten (cl) the left thin locknut (or big axle nut) down against the washer and cone. This may tighten up the cone on the bearings. If it does, use two spanners, one backing the left cone (c-cl) and one tightening (cl) the left thin locknut. When you have the cone and thin locknut set so that the wheel spins smoothly but doesn't wiggle from side to side, tighten (cl) the big nut.

For you *quick-release* people, who have been standing there with your wheel in your hand, now it's your turn. Tightening the cones will take two spanners. You are going to have to work simultaneously on both ends of the axle, and that can get *confusing*. If you have a nut on each end of an axle and you want to loosen them both, you of course turn them both counterclockwise. But you find yourself turning the wrenches in opposite directions. Stand a tolerant friend directly in front of you, face to face, take your *right* foot and kick your friend in the shin. Notice that you've kicked his *left* shin. It's the same problem. It doesn't seem to make sense unless you take the time to look at each thing in its own perspective. Remember when following the directions that "clockwise" or "counterclockwise" are from the perspective of looking at the nut from the same end of the axle that the nut is on, not through the spokes from the opposite side. But it's even more confusing than that. Each threaded end of the axle is going to have not one but two threaded parts on it, a cone and a locknut [see Illustration 23]. To screw or unscrew any one thing on the axle, you have to first go

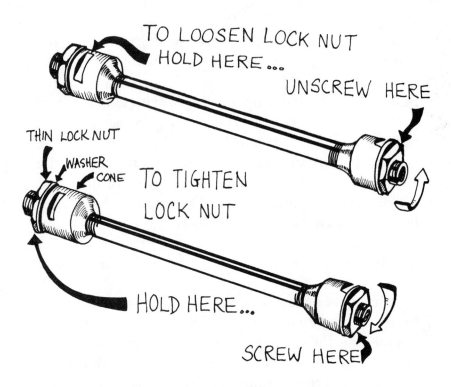

TO LOOSEN LOCK NUT
HOLD HERE...

UNSCREW HERE

THIN LOCK NUT
WASHER
CONE

TO TIGHTEN
LOCK NUT

HOLD HERE...

SCREW HERE

Illustration **23**
TIGHTENING AND LOOSENING A RIGHT LOCKNUT

to the other end and tighten the two things there into each other. Then you can use one of them to hold the axle steady while you screw the thing you originally wanted to screw. Now all this sounds confusing, but it shouldn't prevent you from doing what you want to do. If you enjoy exercising yourself on mind bogglers, you can study Illustration 23 until you grasp "the concept." Or you can just make a point of following the directions very carefully, doing each step as you read it. Don't read the section like a newspaper, without looking at a bike, unless you want to blow your mind.

First check for looseness. Is either of the cone-washer-locknut sets loose, not locked together? Let's say the left one is loose. Put one spanner on the thin locknut on the right end of the axle, and tighten (cl) the left cone until it is snug against the bearings. Back the left cone off (c-cl) until the wheel spins easily, or about ½ turn. Then, still holding the spanner on the right thin locknut, tighten down the left thin locknut onto the cone.

If this process tightens up the left cone on the bearings, put a spanner on the right cone, and back off (c-cl) the left thin locknut. Back (c-cl) the left cone off the bearings, bring the left thin locknut in snug against the washer and cone, and do a two-spanner tighten, so the three left side parts are locked together well. Try the wheel. It has to spin smoothly but not wiggle from side to side. If it's too loose or too tight, take heart and try, try again. If no amount of patience will get the wheel so that it glides smoothly without being loose, you have bearing problems. It's hub overhaul time.

1, 3, 10. *To overhaul a hub,* first remove the wheel from the bike. [See *Wheel Removal* for help] If the wheel is a rear one from a 1 speed or 3 speed bike, take it to a good shop for overhaul—special tools and know-how are needed. If it is a 10 speed rear wheel, go to *Rear Sprocket, remove the freewheel.* When you have removed the freewheel, you can treat the hub like a front wheel hub. If the wheel was held in the drop-outs by a quick-release lever, unscrew (c-cl) the lever, take the unit out of the wheel, then screw it (cl) together again so you don't lose those little springs.

For a short exposition on the subject of getting confused while working on both ends of an axle, turn back a couple of pages (in *loose cones*) and read the first paragraph of *quick-release.* Start the overhaul by putting one thin spanner on the right cone, and another spanner on the right thin locknut (use the big axle nut as a locknut if your hub has no thin locknuts). Lock the right nut against the right cone and washer. From now on, you want that cone-washer-locknut set to stay put.

Lay the wheel down with the right end of the axle resting on a clean rag. Reach under the wheel and put a spanner on the right cone. Put another spanner on the left locknut and unscrew it (c-cl) all the way up off the axle. Now unscrew (c-cl) the left cone up off the end of the axle. Put the parts in a jar as they come off. If there is a dust cap (a ring of thin, often shiny metal pushed into the hub casing [see Illustration 22], pry it out gently with a screwdriver. Often, to get the dust cap out, you have to pick the wheel up and pull the axle down part way—*not* all the way, just far enough that you can slip a screwdriver into the axle hole in the dust cap and pry it out. Work around and around the dust cap as you pry it out, to keep from bending it.

Count the bearings in the left side of the hub. Write the number here   . Do the bearings fill the cup in a circle? If there are big gaps between them, some are missing. There should be only a small amount of extra space between the bearings.

Hold the right end of the axle in the hub so the bearings on that side won't jump out and run away, then turn the wheel over and dump the left side bearings out. To complete the left side bearing dump, get a small magnet or a finger into the left cup and probe out any recalcitrant bearings. Put all the left side bearings in the jar before they can run off and hide from you.

Turn the wheel back over on its right side and slide the axle out. Dump the right side bearings on the clean rag. Complete the dump with a magnet or finger. Count the bearings and write the number here
If it's not the same number that you had on the left side, you're missing some bearings somewhere. Capture

all the balls in the jar. Remove the right side dust cap if there is one.

Clean all the parts in the jar, and the cups that are in the hub; soak the parts in solvent. Examine all the bearing surfaces. Look closely at the shiny rings on the cones and cups where the balls roll. Are there rows of tiny pits? Are the ball bearings discolored? Do your balls have pitted patches (Ouch!) Is the axle stripped of its threads in places? If you have to replace any of the hub parts, it is best to get a whole new set of cones, ball bearings, washers, locknuts and axle. If you get new parts, lock one new cone-washer-locknut set on the new axle in exactly the same place the old axle had its right cone-washer-locknut set. Whatever replacement parts you get, try to match the brand name, and make sure the replacements are *identical* to the old ones. Get extra ball bearings for the ones that may run off and hide; they are shy little fellows, so you have to figure on losing a few.

Begin the hub *reconstruction* by putting the right dust cap over the left end of the axle. Slide it down like a collar over the right cone, so that it will be in position to put in the right side of the hub casing. Remember that whatever you put into the hubs—bearings, grease, cones, etc.—has to be spotlessly clean, no water, grit or solvent on it. Put the wheel down on its left side and spread light bicycle grease around in the right cup. Not too much. Extra grease attracts grit (you can use oil if you are fastidious and want the least possible friction, but oil has to be replenished frequently). Push the axle part way into the hub. Stick the right number of ball bearings in the grease around the inside of the cup. There should be only slight spaces between the ball bearings.

Slide the axle all the way into the hub until the right cone rests on the bearings. Push the right dust cap (if you have one) into the hub casing. Pick up the wheel and hold the axle in place as you turn the wheel over and rest it on the right end of the axle.

Put grease in the left cup and stick the right number of ball bearings in the grease. Screw the left cone down (cl) the axle until it is snug against the ball bearings. Push the dust cap into the left side of the housing. Put the left washer on the axle, and screw the left thin locknut on (cl). Pick up the wheel and give it a spin, holding the axle. If there is slippage back and forth on the axle, the ball bearings may be stacking up in the cups; the little buggers are still putting up a fight in there. Put the wheel down flat and jiggle and twist the axle until your balls get in line. Heh. Screw in (cl) the left cone until it is snug against the bearings, then back it off ½ turn and tighten (cl) the locknut against it. Remember the bearings should be tight enough that there is no wiggle, but loose enough that the wheel spins freely.

If it's a 10 speed rear hub, put some oil or plumbers' thread goop (like Never-seez) on the threads and replace the freewheel carefully, making *sure* you don't strip the threads. If it is a quick-release hub, stick the pole of the unit with a spring around it into the left end of the axle. Put the other spring on the cone end of the quick-release pole, and screw (cl) the cone onto the pole. The narrow ends of the quick-release springs should point toward the center of the hub.

Replace the wheel in the drop-outs. Align your nice smoothly running wheel. If big axle nuts hold the wheel and act as locknuts too, check the cone adjustment when the big nuts are tight. Loosen the left cone if necessary. Whew! Your wheel rolls smooth now. Spin it a time or two. What a marvel of free-flow it is now! Well worth the trouble.

Spokes and Rims

(cl) means clockwise, and usually tightens a nut or bolt. (c-cl) means counterclockwise, and usually loosens.

1, 3, 10. DESCRIPTION: Spokes are the lacy wires that miraculously hold the thin metal rim in a round shape. The spokes are stuck through holes in the flanges of the hub, and these holes are often beveled to accommodate the curve of the spoke at its head end. The bevel or countersink of each spoke hole in the hub is *not* for the head of the spoke to settle down into. It is for the curve of the spoke. The head of the spoke should be on the opposite side of the hub flange from the countersink. The threaded tail end of the spoke disappears into a spoke nipple, which has flat sides and can be tightened (cl) or loosened (c-cl) with a spoke wrench [see Illustration 24]. Each spoke nipple fits through a hole in the *rim*. There are many different sizes and kinds of spokes, including chromed ones, "rustless" steel ones, piano wire ones, stainless steel ones, and butted ones (thicker at the ends where the stress is greater). All the spokes on any one wheel should be tightened to very nearly the same tension. If all the spokes are not the same size or kind, it is difficult to keep their tension even.

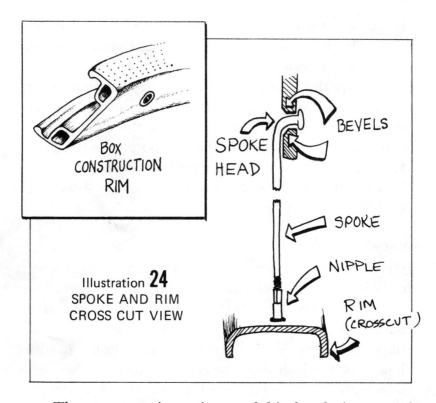

BOX
CONSTRUCTION
RIM

SPOKE
HEAD

BEVELS

SPOKE

NIPPLE

RIM
(CROSSCUT)

Illustration **24**
SPOKE AND RIM
CROSS CUT VIEW

There are various sizes and kinds of rims—steel ones of various shapes, aluminum alloy ones of various shapes, and some very special tubular alloy ones which have insets in them for strength and resilience. Some rims have seams running all the way around their circumferences, others, known as "seamless" rims, are tubular or "box construction" and have only one joint where the ends of the tube meet. Seamless or tubular rims are stronger than seamed ones made of comparable materials. No matter how fancy your rim is, though, *it is fragile.* It takes very little to destroy the miraculous roundness of a rim. Sometime when you're in a bike shop, buy a single spoke of any size. Take it in your hands and bend it. Pretty easy, isn't it? Now think of all the strain rims have to take. It can't be emphasized too much. *Spokes and rims are fragile.*

PROBLEMS: *Rim wobbles.* I hope, after reading the above description, you won't be surprised to find, at times, that you have a wobbly wheel. Perfectly round or "true" rims are rare. Truing a wheel is a high art. Even getting a rim nearly round and evenly tightened so it will last is an art. Bending a rim takes no art or effort at all.

When your wheel wobbles, spin it, if it will spin at all. See how much it wobbles by watching it at the brake shoes, or, if you have hub brakes, at a stay. If it wobbles less than ½ inch from side to side, and not at all up and down, you might have a chance of getting it tolerably straight. To locate the worst wobbles, you can put a felt pen against each brake shoe, so the tip is very close to the rim, then spin the wheel; marks will appear where the rim bends toward the brake on each side.

Look at the rim itself. Is the main point of wobble a little outward flare or bump in the rim—a blip, as it is called? [See Illustration 25] Look at the blip. Is there a blip on both sides of the rim at the same point? Is the blip caused by the joint of a seamless or tubular rim? If your blip is small, not large enough that it misshapes the general roundness of the rim, you might have a pretty good chance of getting it out. But if you have a big blip, or more than ½ inch of side to side wobble, or a bad blip at the joint of the rim, or any up and down "hop" at all, *don't mess with that wheel.* Don't think you can fix things by tightening a spoke here or loosening one there. Take that blipped, wobbly, or egg-shaped wheel to a reliable shop. Ask them if they can save it. Don't hesitate to get a new rim, or even a new wheel if they suggest it. Face the music. Next time have more respect for the fragile nature of a spoked wheel, and steer clear of pot-holes, storm drains, and curbs.

If your blip isn't too bad, or your wobble not too great, there is hope.

1, 3, 10. If you have a *blip or a blip and a wobble,* take care of the blip first. And remember, before you start, that you are not going to be able to make your wheel perfectly round. You are going to try to make it usable. First let the air out of the tire. For most tires, with the standard Schrader valve, push in the little point in the valve trunk to let all the air out of the tire. You may have a Presta valve, which has a threaded point with a tiny metal cap on it that sticks out of the end of the valve trunk. [See Illustration 27] To let the air out, unscrew (c-cl) the tiny cap all the way up the little threaded point until it stops, then push the threaded point in.

Get out your vise-grip (don't use any other tool) and open the jaws so that they are open wide enough to fit around the width of the rim when the handles of the vise-grip are *clamped shut.* Stick the vise-grip between the spokes of the wheel at the point where you have the blip [see Illustration 25]. Center the blip in the jaws of the vise-grip and adjust the jaws so that they will *just barely* hold onto the blip when the handles of the tool are locked closed. Now stop. You have, at your finger-tips, potential for the total destruction of the roundness of your rim. Look closely at what you are about to do. Are there blips on both sides of the rim? The vise-grip will squeeze equally from both sides. If you have a larger blip on one side than on the other, squeeze both sides of the rim until the little blip side is flat. Then take a small, thin piece of wood, like a popsicle stick, and put it along the flattened side of the rim. Adjust the jaws of the vise-grip so that they accommodate the popsicle stick when the handles are snapped all the way closed. Then release the little trip-lever that is on one

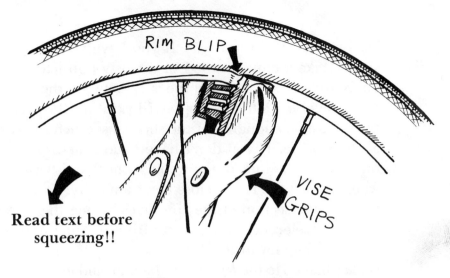

RIM BLIP

VISE GRIPS

Read text before squeezing!!

Illustration **25** SQUEEZING A BLIP

of the vise-grip handles, and, as you keep the jaws barely gripping the rim with one hand, tighten (cl) the adjusting knob of the vise-grip so the jaws move closer to the rim. Turn the knob about ½ turn and squeeze the handles together. Watch the rim, looking at it from a tangent. If the blip is still sticking out, tighten the vise-grip adjusting knob again, ½ turn or less, and squeeze slowly. Watch as you squeeze. Stop squeezing if you're going to go too far before the vise-grip locks. *Keep in mind that you can't unsqueeze the rim!* When the blip has been squeezed in even with the rest of the rim, don't be surprised if there are two small dents on either side of where the blip was. They won't hurt your braking like the blip. Spin the wheel and check for wobble. Wobble often comes along with a blip.

1, 3, 10. To correct a *minor wobble*, first let the air out of your tire. When trying to fix a wobble, you need to have a good reference point on at least one side of the rim. If you have hand brakes, either side-pull or center-pull, you have built-in reference points. Tighten the brakes with an adjusting sleeve if your brake system has one [see Illustration 5]. If you have no adjusting sleeve, take a chip of wood or a trusty popsicle stick, apply the brakes, and jam the stick between the brake hand lever and the post [see Illustration 3], so the brakes are on enough that the shoes just touch the rim at the wobble. If you don't have hand brakes, loosen one of the axle nuts of the wobbly wheel and twist the wheel so that the rim is close to a frame stay. You want to move the section of the rim that's hitting the brake (or other reference point) away from it. For instance, to move the rim to the *left, tighten* (cl) the nipples of spokes that go to the *left* side of the hub, and *loosen* (c-cl) the nipples of the spokes that go to the *right* side of the hub. [See Illustration 26]

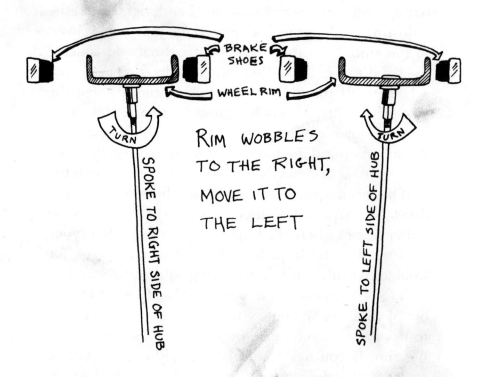

Illustration **26** STRAIGHTENING A MINOR WOBBLE

Before you start wildly tightening and loosening spoke nipples, consider a few things. The ideal wheel has exactly the same amount of tension on every spoke. So, in your adjusting, don't leave any spoke completely loose, and don't tighten any one spoke in order to do all the rim moving. Think of a wobble as the result of a group of six or eight maladjusted spokes (not just one individualist, but a maladjusted minority— probably student spokes, whose nipples were always permissive). To move the rim laterally, you are going to want to adjust the whole group of six or eight nipples. If any of the spokes in the group you are working on are obviously much too tight or much too lose, you have to try to bring them into the same range of tightness as the other spokes in the group. You have to learn to get the "feel" of the median tension on the spokes. One way to try to get that feel is to go around the whole wheel, tightening and loosening every spoke about 1/10 of a turn. You might find, right away, that all or most of the nipples are frozen to the spokes and very difficult to turn. If your wheel has frozen nipples (a very uncomfortable condition, I'm sure), take it to a pro. *Don't mess with it.*

You will find on any rim that even in the straight sections there may be variations of tension on the spokes. This is especially true of rear wheels. The rear wheels of many bicycles are flattened or "dished" to compensate for the sprockets being on one side.

If you have a 10 speed, look straight down on the rear wheel from above. Notice that the spokes go out farther to the hub on the left side. The amount of dish necessary for most 5 and 10 speed bikes is so great that it should actually be done through the use of slightly shorter spokes on the sprocket side of the hub. Sad to say, very few rear wheels are made with shorter spokes on the right side. Dishing is usually done by just tightening all the spokes of the right side of the rear wheel. And for some reason it just never comes out quite as strong that way. But even on a normal front wheel, you are likely to find some spokes that are tightened up much more than others. So, as you try to take a wobble out, remember that you are not trying to make a perfect wheel. You are trying to cause a general movement of the rim without putting too much or too little tension on any one spoke.

Get the spokes in the area of your wobble into the same range of tightness as those of the rest of the wheel. One aid in doing this might be found in the spoke threads. Look closely at your spokes where they disappear into the nipples. If there are any threads showing, the number of threads should be very nearly equal on each spoke. The exception is a 10 speed rear wheel, where all the left side spokes should be equal and all the right side spokes shorter (fewer threads showing) than the left but equal among themselves. On 10 speed rear wheels the right side spokes will be tightened more than the left side by about a full turn.

When the spokes are all in the same range of tightness, look again at the wobble. Loosen the spokes to the same side of the hub as the wobble and tighten the spokes to the opposite side of the hub from the wobble [see Illustration 26]. Adjust the whole group of six or eight spokes at the wobble, then check to see how much you've changed things. Be careful that you don't generate secondary wobbles on the ends of your original wobble. Tighten and loosen more in the middle of the wobble than at the ends. When you think you have removed the wobble, readjust the brakes, spin the wheel, and apply the brakes slowly. If the wobble isn't too bad, don't worry. The earth is slightly pear-shaped, and it has been spinning pretty well for quite a while. If your wobble is still too bad, or if the one big wobble has become several bothersome small ones, try again with a light touch and lots of patience. If your patience is running out, *quit now!* Go do something else.

When your patience is restored and you try again to get a little more roundness into your wheel, you may find that it just plays tricks on you. Wobbles appear where moments before there was only straightness. One big wobble turns into three little ones. That sort of thing. It can get like the scene in *Fantasia* with Mickey Mouse and the multiplying brooms. With a great deal of experience, you will learn that elusive feel of spoke tension that controls all these secondary wobbles. But if you are a beginner, try to get the wheel tolerably straight. If you don't like tolerating little wobbles, take the wheel to a first-rate shop and have them true it. Make sure you patronize a first-rate shop. Many shops have people truing wheels who know very little more about it than you. A good shop will have a wheel expert who does all the wheel truing. It will cost you something, but the wheel will stay nearly straight for some time.

If they tell you that you have to replace the rim, or the whole wheel, do so if you can possibly afford to. Just make sure you are getting equipment that's as good as the stuff you replace. If you have Campagnolo hubs, for instance, don't replace them with anything but the same. They last almost forever, and are so steep that it's usually much cheaper to keep your old hub and have the shop respoke it with a nice new rim.

Check for spokes sticking through a new or straightened rim before you re-inflate the tire. Put a finger under the rubber or cloth rim strip and run it all the way around the wheel. If there are spoke points sticking up more than 1/16 inch, take the wheel off the bike [see *Wheel Removal*] and take the tire off the wheel with tire irons. File down those spoke ends, clean all of those sharp filings off the wheel, replace the rim strip and the tire, and put the wheel back on the bike.

Broken spokes. This includes spokes that are stuck in their nipples and no longer adjustable, so they have to be cut. Clip them with cable clippers or wire cutters —the mashing kind are best—and treat them like other broken spokes.

If you have broken spokes, your wheel might not be worth fixing up. If the rim wobbles a little, replacing the broken spokes and truing out the wobble might be possible. But if the wobble is major and there are more than two or three broken spokes, you are going to have about a 50-50 chance of getting a nearly round wheel. Any blips or dents in the surface of the rim are going to lower your odds. If the bike has foot brakes, no brake pads grab the rim, so your wheel doesn't have to be exactly round; you can try to save it even if it's pretty bad. But if your bike has hand brakes, you want straight rims. Buy a new rim and have a good shop spoke it with new spokes, or buy a whole new wheel, as it doesn't cost much more. An old wheel with some new and some old spokes and a rusty, battered rim is not only dangerous—it is expensive if you have hand brakes that grab the rim and catch on a battered place and consequently wear the tire down in one place.

1, 3, 10. If you have a wheel with just two or three broken spokes and you think it's worth saving, take it off the bicycle [see *Wheel Removal*] and take the tire off the rim [see *Tires, removal*]. Take the broken spokes out of the hub and the rim. If you have a 10 speed rear wheel, chances are the broken spokes are on the side of the hub that's blocked by the cluster of sprockets on your freewheel. To get at the spoke holes on the right side of the hub, you have to remove the freewheel [see *Rear Sprocket, freewheel removal*]. Go take the freewheel off, and then come back here.

Take a good spoke off the wheel and take it, its nipple, and if it's convenient, the whole wheel to a good shop. Make sure the replacements are *exactly* the same length as your old ones, and if possible, the same thickness and made for the same kind of nipple as the old one. Get new nipples if necessary. Make sure the new spokes fit into the spoke holes of your hub.

When you stick a new spoke into the hole in the hub, make sure you stick it through from the opposite direction of the spokes with their heads through the holes on either side. Draw the new spoke through the other spokes in such a way that it will be free to reach the rim without hitting any spokes. You may have to curve the spoke a little to do this, but that's OK; it'll straighten out when it's tightened, as long as you haven't put a sharp bend in it. When you have drawn the spoke all the way in to its head, it will be pointing at the rim, but it will not be pointing at an empty spoke hole in the rim. If you are replacing several spokes, several spoke holes might look right. To find the right hole on the rim, look at the direction of the spokes on the hub. The spokes alternate, one forward, one back. You want your new spoke to go the opposite direction from the ones on either side. Move the spoke through its brothers until it reaches a hole in the rim. If you're not sure that this is the right hole, check to see whether the spoke is about the right length at that hole. When you think you have the right hole, double-check by looking at the spokes that go into the rim on either side of your new one. The pattern should be the same as it is around the rest of the wheel.

When you are sure you have the new spoke aimed at the right hole, check to see if the other spokes on the wheel are laced. On almost all bikes, the spokes cross each other between the hub and the rim. On less expensive wheels, the spokes don't touch where they cross each other. On laced wheels, the spokes touch where they cross. Laced wheels are strong because any road shock coming up a spoke travels through the juncture into a second spoke, and is taken up twice as well. If your wheel is laced, make sure you weave the new spoke through the old ones in such a way that you match exactly the lacing on the rest of the wheel.

Insert a nipple through the right hole for your new, correctly laced spoke. Spin the nipple onto the spoke (cl) and tighten it with your fingers.

Repeat the procedure for any other broken spokes. Replace your sprocket cluster (cl) if you are working on a 10 speed rear wheel, then turn to *Tire* and *Wheel Replacement* to get your bike back in one piece. True the wheel [see *minor wobble* above], and you're all set.

Tires

(cl) means clockwise, and usually tightens a nut or bolt. (c-cl) means counterclockwise, and usually loosens.

1, 3, 10. DESCRIPTION AND DIAGNOSIS:
The rubber thing on the wheel that's supposed to stay full of air. There are two basic types: clinchers (sometimes called wire-ons) have separate inner tubes; sew-ups (tubulars) incorporate the tire and tube in one unit. Sew-ups are generally much lighter and able to take much more pressure than clinchers. But they are delicate, difficult to repair, and more expensive than

clinchers. All sew-up tires have Presta valves, and some clincher tires have them too. But most common clincher tire tubes now have Schrader valves, which are similar to the tire valves on cars [see Illustration 27]. Any tire has a recommended pressure. The tire *must* be ridden *only* with that amount of air pressure in it. Many riders, especially sew-up users, carry pressure gauges which fit over the valve stems. Riders with clincher tires can often learn to "feel" when the tire is hard enough.

There's a great *curb-edge test* you can do to make sure your tires are inflated just right. Rest the wheel on the edge of a curb or stair, so the bike sticks out into the street or path, perpendicular to the curb or stair edge. Get the wheel so you can push down on it at about a 45 degree angle from above the bike. Push hard on the handlebars or seat, depending on which wheel you're testing. The curb should flare the tire a bit but shouldn't push right through the tire and clunk against the rim. You want the tire to have a little "give" when you ride over chuckholes and rocks, in other words,

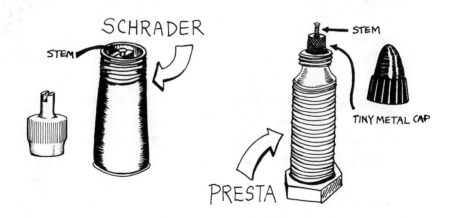

Illustration **27** TWO DIFFERENT TIRE VALVES

but you don't want it so soft that you bottom out. If you are a hot-shot who wants tires so hard that they don't have any give, you'll have to stick to riding on clean-swept Velodrome tracks, or watch very carefully for little sharp objects on the road. Or you'll have to get used to that sudden riding-on-the-rim feeling that follows the blowout of an overblown tire.

PROBLEMS: *Tire soft.* Pump it up. Don't waste your precious energy riding around on soft tires. They can take the fun out of any ride, even a casual jaunt down to the corner for a beer. To pump up tires with Schrader valves, screw on or push on the pump chuck (the thing that fits over the valve). Sometimes the screw-on type lets all the air out as you screw them on; if that's the case, get a new chuck with a lever for your pump. The lever type lets all the air out if you push them on too far, so push them on just far enough so they get a good grip on the valve when you clamp the lever down. That way you'll be able to get the chuck off without letting much air out.

Make sure the tire is seated, by checking the bead all the way around the tire on both sides, then pump until the tire feels tight to the squeeze. Release the lever and get the chuck off as fast as you can, so no air can leak out. Check the pressure by the *curb-edge test* above.

To inflate a sew-up or a fancy clincher with a Presta valve, unscrew the tiny cap on the valve, press it to make sure it's loose, then push on the chuck of the pump, making sure it goes on far enough so the rubber ring in the chuck is past the tiny cap and down on the trunk of the valve. Go easy as you push it on and also as you pump, especially with those frame-mounted hand-pumps, or you might break the valve. Hold the part of the pump next to the chuck firmly with one hand as you pump with the other, and cock the thumb of the pump-holding hand against the rim of the wheel for good leverage. Pumpa, pumpa, pumpa, till sweat beads your brow. Use the *curb-edge test* above, when you think you've got the tire hard. It always takes more pumpa, pumpa and cussa, cussa than you think it will.

To inflate a Schrader valve tire, or a Presta valve tire with an adapter at a gas station, *be careful!!!* Many gas stations have compressors that are made to fill truck tires up to 150 pounds per square inch or more. That kind of pressure can blow any bike tire clean away! Park or lean your bike by the pump, out of the cars' way, and so it is standing up. Spin the tire you need to fill until the valve is down at the bottom of the wheel. That way you can use the fitting on the end of the pump chuck and push down on it for a tight, accurate fit. When the chuck is on tight, squeeze the pump trigger just a *tiny bit* at a time. Little squirts of air should go in, almost like the poofs from a hand pump. Check the tire often, to make sure it isn't getting too hard. Check the bead all around on both sides of the rim, to make sure it isn't about to bulge up, allowing a huge bubble of tube to bloop out and explode in your face. When you think you've got the tire hard enough, do a careful *curb-edge test,* as above, before you ride away.

Flat. Flats are due to either slow leaks, quick leaks, or blowouts. No matter what kind of flat you have, *don't ride the bike on a flat tire! Or even a soft tire!* The tire, the rim, and your life are at stake. Even pushing the bike along on a flat is bad for the tube. When you get a flat, carry the bike until you can fix it or have it fixed.

Check the valve first. Pump up the tire. Spit or put a little water on your fingertip and put it lightly over the end of the valve. If little bubbles come through the water, see *Valve stem is loose.*

If your *clincher tire is flat,* take the wheel off the bike according to the *wheel removal* procedure. Then let all the air out of the tire (if there is any air in it) by pushing the stem top in if it's a Schrader valve, or by unscrewing the metal cap and then pushing in the stem tip if you have a Presta valve [see Illustration 27].

Use your bare hands whenever you can in removing and replacing a tire. Check to see how tight the tire is on the rim by running your fingers all the way around the wheel between the tire and the rim. This will break the tire loose if it's stuck anywhere, and give you a good idea of how tough it's going to be to remove. If the tire is quite loose, grab it with both hands in one place and pull away from the center of the wheel, so that one bead (the inner edge [see Illustration 28]) of the tire stretches up. Lift that stretch-up place over the rim, and then work your way around the wheel, spreading the section of bead that has been pulled over the rim. This will be possible only if the tire is a loose-fitting one.

If the tire is so tight that you can't pull a section of the bead over the rim, use your tire irons. Do *not* use a screwdriver or any other substitute. Stick the round end of the tire iron a little way under one of the beads of the tire. Make sure you aren't getting both beads of the tire, with the tube pinched in between. Pinching the tube can easily put a hole in it, even if you are using tire irons. When you have the iron under one bead of the tire, pry the iron all the way out and down and hook the handle end of it on a spoke [see Illustration 28]. With a second iron, pry out more of the bead a couple of inches from your first pry. If you need to make a third pry, do it about 3 inches farther down the line, but usually two pries will get the tire bead well on its way. When the tire bead is on its way, in other

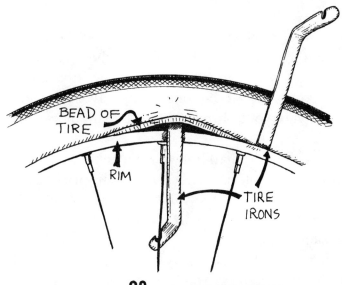

Illustration **28** USING TIRE IRONS

words, when it doesn't try to jump back onto the rim, take all the tire irons out, stick one iron between the popped-out bead and the rim, and peel the rest of the bead out of the rim. You've now got the tire half off the rim, and you shouldn't take it any farther off.

Pull the tube out of the tire on the side that has the bead out of the rim, *except* where it is held by the valve. Leave the valve in the rim and most of the tube out of the rim and out of the tire. Pump up the tube until it swells to about 1½ times its normal size. If you can't pump up the tube, the leak is pretty big and the tube should be replaced. If the tube fills up, look for the leak. When you find it, mark it on the tube. Push the tube back next to the tire and look at the tire and rim of the wheel where the puncture is. Look for tacks or pieces of glass or sharp pieces of metal stuck in the tire, or a sharp burr in the rim, or a sharp spoke tail sticking through the rim strip. When you have found and removed or filed down the cause of your tube leak, you can completely deflate the tube. To get the valve out of the hole in the rim, first unscrew the cap and sleeve around the valve if you have either, then pull a section of *the bead that you have already removed* back over to the opposite side of the tube at the valve. Now you can slip the valve out of the hole in the rim by pulling on the tube.

If you have a small hole in your tube, you can patch it. But if the hole is larger than a pin-prick, or if the leak is at the base of the valve, replace the tube. Many shops replace any tube with a leak. They quote Webster, who states that a patch is a "temporary repair." They say that their shops do only permanent repairs. They have a good point. You can get fairly inexpensive tubes. But if you have a small puncture in your tube, and you don't mind the idea of temporary repairs (what isn't temporary, you might ask in response to Webster), get a bicycle tube patching kit and follow its instructions. Different kits have different methods, but the general procedure is simple.

Clean and dry the tube, then scrape it with an abrasive, like the scraper on the lid of the patch kit, or a piece of sandpaper. Spread a thin, even film of glue all around the hole, making sure that the area you cover is bigger than the patch you're going to use. Wipe off any thick globs, or they won't dry and seal up tight.

When the whole area of glue turns from shiny to that dull-surface color that means it's dry (it only takes a minute or so), peel the backing off the patch and stick it in place, without touching the glue or the sticky side of the patch. Pinch and knead the patched tube between your fingers, starting at the center of the patch and working out to the edges. Squeeze it as hard as your fingers can. When the patch is stuck on there, take a little fine dust or talcum powder or something, and poof it around the patch, so the extra glue on the tube won't stick to the inside of the tire or wheel. Replace the tube and tire and it will be ready for immediate use.

If you decide to replace your leaky tube with an inexpensive one, you should check the valve stem of your new tube. Pump up the tube until it is 1½ times its normal size, then spit or put a little water on your fingertip and put your fingertip loosely over the end of the valve.

If little bubbles come out between your fingertip and the valve, the *valve stem is loose.* To tighten it, you need either a fancy stem tool that you can buy at a bike shop, or one of the metal valve caps that have two prongs on top of them [see Illustration 27]. A bike shop might give you one of those, or sell it to you for very little. When you have a valve tool or metal valve cap with the prongs, stick the prongs down the valve trunk and turn them back and forth until you feel them slip over the little arms of the stem. Now tighten (cl) the stem. Not too hard, especially if you have the fancy tool. Those stems are delicate. Try the wet finger test again. If there are bubbles, you might have a lemon of a tube. The store might replace it, if you're lucky.

To replace the clincher tube and tire, start by letting almost all the air out of the tube. If you are putting in a new tube, put just a little bit of air in it so it isn't flat and unworkable. If you are putting on a new tire, get one of the beads around the rim, using your bare hands *only.* If you can't get the tire bead on, it's the wrong size. It might be hard to get the last inches of the bead over the rim, but puff and cuss and get it on by hand.

You have one tire bead in the rim and one bead off the edge of the rim. Push the tire from the side that has the bead off the rim over to the opposite side of the hole in the rim for the tube valve. Put the valve in and

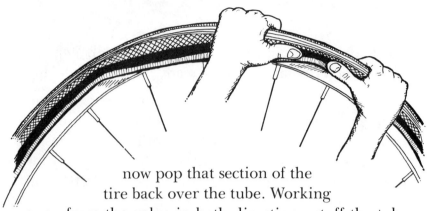

now pop that section of the tire back over the tube. Working away from the valve in both directions, stuff the tube up into the tire and over onto the rim. Then work the remaining tire bead over the lip of the rim with your thumbs, making sure the tube doesn't get pinched between the tire bead and the rim. When you get down to the last few inches of the tire bead, it will get tough. Roll up your sleeves. Make sure the tube is tucked up onto the rim where it won't get pinched and that almost all the air is out of it. Work with both thumbs on one part of the remaining bead at a time; don't try to pop the whole thing over at once until you have only about 1 or 2 inches left. Use your hands and have at it. Don't slam the wheel around in your excitement—wheels bend easily. And *don't* use a screwdriver, or, if you can possibly avoid it, even the tire iron. Anything that you stick under the tire at this juncture could reach inside the rim, grab the tube and pinch it. So use your hands and your patience and your perseverance. Franz Kafka once said, "There is only one human sin—impatience." Not that I expect you to keep your patience when that tire bead bites your finger, then jumps off the rim. When you've just got to throw something, don't throw the wheel. Grab a handy wrench and throw it. It will make a much more satisfying clang, and it won't bend. Just be careful where you throw it.

When you get the tire over the rim, first push the valve in and out of the rim a couple of times to make sure the tube isn't pinched between the tire bead and the rim right next to the valve. Then go have a beer or indulge in whatever relaxes you. When you are restored, come back and pump up the tire. If it goes flat, do the wet finger test on the valve. If the valve is OK, it must be the tube. Call the tire and tube what they are, and start all over. I know exactly how you feel. If the tire holds air, replace the wheel [see *Wheel Replacement*], then celebrate with another relaxer and a restorer too.

10. If you have a *flat sew-up or tubular tire,* let me put my cards on the table. I think sew-ups are for racing or very, very specialized road riding. I don't use sew-ups on my own ride-around-town bike. Sew-ups cost more and are more vulnerable, so if you can afford that kind of luxury, I recommend you have a pro fix your flat sew-ups. Or if you want to master the art, most sew-up patch kits have adequate instructions.

Whether you take your sew-ups to a shop or patch them yourself, you'll want to be able to take them off the rim and put them back. *To remove a sew-up from the rim,* push it with your fingers off one side of the rim, being careful to keep the glued-on rim strip stuck to the tire. When the tire is all removed except the valve stem, pull the stem straight out of its hole in the rim.

To mount a sew-up on the rim, completely deflate the tire and stretch it gently. Make a figure 8 out of it and hook one loop under a crooked knee. Stick an arm through the other loop and slip it over your shoulder. Stretch it gently, until you hear a tiny crickly-crackly noise of the casing expanding, then *stop* stretching. Take it off before it breaks or twaps you. Spread an even film of rim cement around the rim and let it dry until it is tacky. Put the tire valve in its hole, and work around the rim away from the valve with both hands, pushing the tire onto the rim with your thumbs in such a way that the tire goes on evenly and you don't get glue on yourself, the tire, or the outside of the rim. That's a trick. Work slowly. Put on the section of the tire that's opposite the valve last, trying to keep the tension even all the way around, so the valve isn't pulled one way or the other. When the tire is on, pump it up partially so it assumes its normal shape. Then go around the wheel, lifting, moving and reseating the portions of the tire that are to one side or the other. Spin the wheel to check for trueness of the tire. Trueness is very important, because any tire wobble will cause excessive wear. When you are satisfied with the trueness of the tire, pump it up so it's good and hard, and leave it for at least ½ day to let the glue dry before you ride on it. Riding on a sew-up that has wet glue can

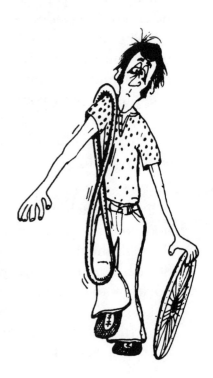

make for a very oddly shaped tire. While you're waiting for the glue to dry, it might be a good idea to wipe off that unavoidable extra that somehow gets on the outside of the rim, or the tire, or you. Fancy bike shops sell a solvent made just for the purpose. Don't use any other solvent; you might ruin the tires or the braking surface of the rim.

To keep sew-up flats to a minimum, I recommend the little tire saver gizmos that graze along the surface of the tire and pull out anything that gets picked up by your tires. Most punctures in tires are caused not when a sharp object is first hit, but when it works its way through the rubber and cloth casing into the tube after many successive revolutions of the wheel. To help avoid unexpected blow-outs, let a little pressure out of each tire after you finish a ride. But don't forget to pump up before the next ride.

The Frame Is The
Heart and Soul of The Bicycle

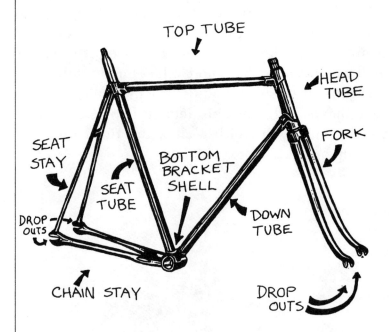

Illustration **29** FRAME

8. Frame

(cl) means clockwise, and usually tightens a nut or bolt. (c-cl) means counterclockwise, and usually loosens.

1, 3, 10. DESCRIPTION: The frame consists of a horizontal top tube, a head tube at the front of the bike, a seat tube parallel to the head tube under the seat, a diagonal down tube from the head to the bottom bracket, chain stays from the bottom bracket to the rear drop-outs, and seat stays from the rear drop-outs to the top of the seat tube [see Illustration 29].

The frame is more than it might seem. It is not just a diamond and two triangles of tubing brazed or welded together. It is the heart and soul of a bicycle. It is not just the most expensive part of a bike. It is the single most significant part in determining the quality of a bike. The frame is also the single most difficult part to repair. When you are looking at a bike you want to buy, look at the frame first. Is it made of good tubing? Columbus, Reynolds 531, Ishiwata, and Falk double-butted are among the best. Double-butted tubing is thin and springy and light in the middle, and thicker and stronger at the ends, where the stress is. There are too many other good types of tubing for everyday bikes to list here. Then there are the frames made of welded tubing that is very heavy, and really should have been left to do the plumbing.

To distinguish good from bad tubing, first pick up the bike. If it weighs a ton, that usually means that its tubes are thick to make up for their weakness. If the bike is light, put it upright on a flat surface and stand to one side of it. Make sure the tires are inflated to the proper pressure. Grab the handlebar nearest you with one hand, and the seat with the other. Hold the bike firmly and tilt it away from you. Put one foot *gently* on the end of the bottom bracket axle. Give a *light* push with your toe. Go easy; one quick way to alienate a bike dealer is to start kicking and shoving his bikes around. When you push lightly with your toe, the frame should flex slightly, then spring back. If you want to educate your toe to the right feel, try the bottom bracket push test on a super-expensive racing machine. Tiny bit of give, quick spring-back. Feel it? Try the same test on a 50 pound balloon tire special. Some difference, isn't there? The balloon tire special either doesn't give at all or gives and then is sluggish in coming back to straight. (Which isn't to say that balloon tire bikes are useless. I have one for beach riding.)

The best test for any frame, of course, is riding the bike. But it's hard to tell how good a bike is on the first ride. If you are an experienced rider, you can trust your "feel" after one ride on a new bike. If you are new to the game, don't rely too heavily on your first impression.

One attribute of a good frame is well-brazed lug joints. The tubes on most good light bikes are brazed into little metal sleeve joints called lugs [see Illustration 30]. Brazing is done at relatively low temperatures, to avoid making the frame tubing brittle. Metal, especially high-carbon bike tube metal, which has been heated to a high temperature and then cooled, tends to fatigue and break quickly. So low-temperature compound is used to attach the frame tubes to the lugs. The brazing is a high art. If you look closely at the edges of any lug on a brazed type bike, you can see the marks

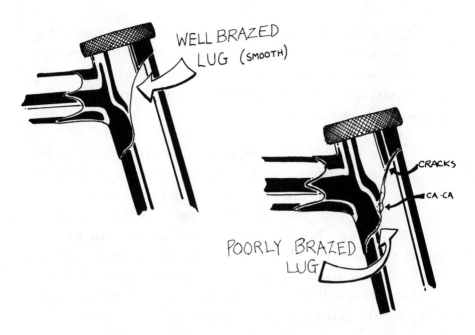

Illustration **30**   LUGS (FRAME JOINTS)

of the artist who did the brazing. If he was great, the joint of the tube and the lug will be perfectly smooth all the way around. Obvious globs of extra around the edges of the lug, or little holidays where you can see a crack back under the lug are the signs of a mediocre frame builder. For more information on the design and construction of frames, read the *Frame* chapter in *Bike Tripping;* the chapter is by Al Eisentraut, who is a great master of the art.

I'm not saying you must buy a frame that's made by a great frame builder. I'm just saying that if you get a not-so-great frame, you have to be kind to it. Any bike, even one with big fat welded joints, will last if you respect it for what it is—good, reliable transportation.

Frame problems, such as a broken joint, a bent or broken tube, or a loss of alignment, are next to impossible to repair. I don't recommend that you try doing it or even having it done. Don't ever try to weld a broken or cracked frame tube. If your frame bends or breaks, you have to get a new frame. So when you buy a bike, buy one with a frame that will do the job you want it to. Then don't expect more of it than you should.

One note about *paint:* new frames have good paint jobs. Keep the original paint on a frame as long as possible. Keep the bike out of the rain and touch up scratches with auto touch-up paint to prevent rust. To repaint a frame you have to take everything off it. If you're up to that, use the various sections of this book that apply. If not, have a good shop do the job. Do-it-yourself painting means: first thoroughly stripping the old paint (use a liquid paint remover). The frame has to be perfectly clean and dry. Then spray on a coat or two of primer, making each coat as smooth as possible and always letting it dry thoroughly before spraying the next coat. Then several coats of spray-on lacquer. Or you can take the bare frame to an auto paint shop and get a bake-on job. You might get it done pretty cheaply if you're willing to have them put the frame through the works with an auto body. Just wait for one that has a color you like.

9. Seat

(cl) means clockwise, and usually tightens a nut or bolt. (c-cl) means counterclockwise, and usually loosens.

1, 3, 10. DESCRIPTION: The seat is the leather or plastic thing you sit on. It is attached by a heavy wire frame and a bracket with tightening nuts to a post. The post is held by a pinned binderbolt in the seat tube of the bike frame. [See Illustration 31] Sizes, shapes, hardnesses, and durabilities of different seats vary widely. If you plan to ride long distances, you should get a quality nylon, leather-covered nylon, or top-grade butt leather seat. The seat brackets which fit on the top end of the seat post are standardized at 7/8 inch. But the o.d.s. (outside diameters) of seat posts where they fit into the seat tube of the bike frame are anything but standardized. They vary from about 7/8 inch to 1-1/8 inch. Often they are calibrated on a metric scale. There are fancy seat posts that incorporate the seat bracket and the post in one unit. These are often adjustable to a much finer degree than the standard seat bracket, but they are also often a good deal heavier. If you have one of these fancy units, and it has the tightening bolts back under the seat where they're hard to get at, you have to get a special Campagnolo wrench to reach in there, or a copy of that wrench, or, in a pinch, you can get a countersunk, box-end, 10 mm wrench; Sears has them.

PROBLEMS: *Seat loose.* If it *tilts forward and back* on the end of the post, get a box end, open end, or crescent wrench that fits the tightening nuts exactly, and tighten them up [cl—see Illustration 31]. Tighten them evenly, doing a few turns on one, then a few on the other, and as you tighten, shift the seat slightly every once in a while to make sure that the bracket is sitting firmly in the position you want. I'm not going to tell you what position that should be. You might be built differently from me. Generally, it's been my experience that many people, especially girls, like their seats tipped forward slightly from level. I happen to like mine tipped back ever so slightly. But the seat should be close to level. If you can't get it to stay in the position you want, I recommend one of the fancy, micro-adjustable seat post-bracket units. Or you might try sliding the seat back or forward in the brackets, loosening and tightening the same nuts that adjust the tilt of the seat. Sliding the seat forward gives you a more sprinty position, back a more relaxed, even-paced position.

1, 3, 10. If your seat *swivels from side to side,* or if the whole post slides down into the frame tube, set the post at the right height for you. I'm not going to tell you what your right height is. Generally, though, people like the seat set at such a level that when they sit on it, they can put the pedal at the bottom of its stroke, stretch their leg out straight, and rest their heel flat on the pedal. Measure pedal length with *your* seat centered on the bike seat so that as you pedal down the road *your* seat doesn't have to rock from side to side on the bike seat, which creates a particularly distressing friction. When you get the seat where you want it, tighten (cl) the binderbolt [see Illustration 31] with a box end wrench if you can get one or an open end wrench that fits well, or a carefully used crescent wrench. If you have a fancy bike with an inset binder-bolt that has a hexagon-shaped hole in it, you have to get an Allen wrench that fits it. You really have to tighten (cl) that binderbolt pretty well, and if you don't have a wrench that fits it, you can bugger the bolt easily. So be firm, but careful. The best approach is to loosen the nut a bunch, put a drop of oil on the bolt threads, then tighten the nut smoothly and thoroughly. If the bolt spins as you turn on the nut, it probably has a stripped pin. Take the nut off, using the vise-grip to hold the bolt if necessary, and take the bolt out. Replace it with an exact duplicate. If the hole in the frame for the pin on the bolt is ruined, you have to resort to a bolt with a hex head that you can hold with a wrench as you tighten the nut up.

If no amount of tightening on the binderbolt will tighten up the frame tube on the seat post, you have a post that's too small for your frame tube. Get a post that's the right size, or get a shim—a thin, curved piece of metal—and put it around the post where the binder-bolt will clamp on it, and then tighten up on the binderbolt.

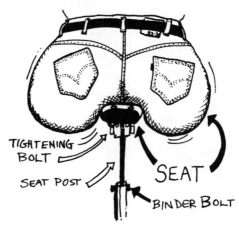

TIGHTENING BOLT

SEAT POST

SEAT

BINDER BOLT

Illustration **31**   SEAT

If, by some chance, you have a post that is too big for your frame tube, don't force it into the tube. It will stretch and weaken the frame at that point. Get a post that fits, or get one that's too small and shim it.

1, 3, 10. *Seat saggy.* You have an old leather seat. When you sit on it, you sink down until your bottom rests on all the wrong places. You want to get the seat tight enough that you rest on the correct place. To stretch the seat tighter, use an open end wrench to tighten (cl) the nut that's on a long bolt under the front end of the seat. If the whole bolt spins, you have to grip it with the vise-grip at the back end of the bolt, or with a pair of pliers at the front end, or with a little open end wrench if the back end of the bolt is squared off. It might be easier if you loosen (c-cl) the tightening nuts on the bracket and take the seat off the bike. Getting an open end wrench around the nut on the long bolt and turning it is a trick. You often have to push the leather back and forth to get the wrench in and out. But have patience and persevere.

10. Power Train

(cl) means clockwise, and usually tightens a nut or bolt.
(c-cl) means counterclockwise, and usually loosens.

1, 3, 10. DESCRIPTION AND DIAGNOSIS:

If the frame of a bicycle is its heart and soul, the power train is the bike's blood and guts. The power train delivers some percentage of the energy that you put into the pedals to the back wheel of your bike. Its front half consists of the pedals, the cranks, the bottom bracket set, perhaps a front changer, and the front sprocket(s) or chainwheel(s). [See Illustrations 32, 33 and 34] Between the front and back halves there is a chain. The back half consists of the rear sprocket(s),

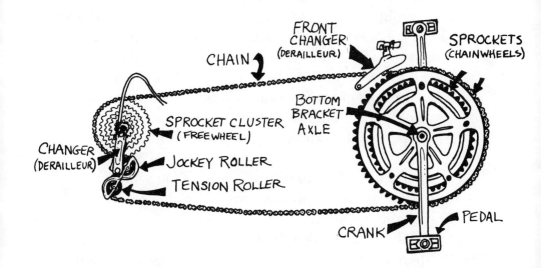

Illustration **32**   10 SPEED POWER TRAIN

and perhaps a 3 speed hub or a derailleur-type changer. The better all of these parts work, the more efficient your system is, and the more of your energy will get to the rear wheel.

1, 3, 10. If there are nasty *grinding, rubbing, squeaking, kerchunking, or clunking noises* when you pedal, you can make an easy test to find out if you have a power train problem. Get going at a good clip on a quiet, level place or a slight downhill grade, then just coast. If the nasty noises do not stop when you stop pedaling, your problem is in the back wheel, not the power train. See *Hub Problems* and check for brake *stickies* under *Brakes, General.* If a nasty noise appears only when you pedal, then see if it repeats itself. If it repeats itself each time your pedal makes a revolution, then it's probably a *Front Half* problem. If it repeats itself once for every two revolutions of your pedal, then you have a chain problem; go directly to *Chain Problems.* If the noise repeats itself two to three times for every revolution of the pedal, then you probably have a back half problem; see *Rear Changer Problems* and *Rear Sprocket Problems.* If the noise is constant, unvarying, you have to find out where it is by listening and watching all the parts of the power train. It's easier and safer to do this sort of observation with the bike up on a rack or floor stand [see *Tools*]. When you think you know which part of the power train is acting up, turn to that section.

If you have 3 or 10 gears (or any number between), a constant noise or problem might be due to a faulty gear changer system.

3. Three speed people: if your *gears slip* or change by themselves, or you can't get into a gear (usually high), or the gear level gets stuck, or you can't get out of a gear at all (usually high), see *Hub Changer.*

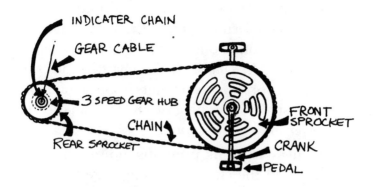

Illustration **33** 3 SPEED POWER TRAIN

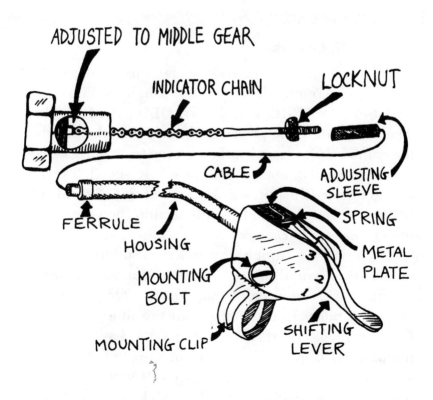

Illustration **34** 3 SPEED LEVER AND CABLE

10. Ten speed people: if the chain comes off the front sprockets, or rubs against the front changer, or you can't get it onto one of the sprockets, see *Front Changer* under *Mechanism.* If the chain comes off the rear sprockets or you can't get it onto one of the sprockets (usually the biggest or the smallest), see *Rear Changer* under *Mechanism.*

If you hear a plunk-plunking noise when you're in low gear and the chain is on the largest of the rear sprockets, STOP RIDING!!! That innocuous little sound is a warning that the rear changer (derailleur) is out of adjustment, and just about to self-destruct in the spokes. See *Rear changer adjustment* to save it (page 184).

Front Half, General

(cl) means clockwise, and usually tightens a nut or bolt. (c-cl) means counterclockwise, and usually loosens.

1, 3, 10. DESCRIPTION AND DIAGNOSIS: The front half of the power train consists of the pedals, the cranks, the bottom bracket set, the front sprocket(s) or chainwheel(s), and, if you have a 10 speed, a front changer [see Illustrations 32, 33 and 34]. The front changer is not included in this section, however, but under *Changer Mechanism.*

If you have a front half problem, you have to find out where it is, and then go to the section on that unit. If your *chain is throwing,* or your *gear is slipping,* or your *changer is rubbing* on the chain all the time, see *Front Changer Problems.* If your chain goes *kerchunk* and jumps each time it hits a certain point of the front sprocket, see *Front Sprocket Problems.* If you hear nasty noises at each revolution of the pedal, first check the pedal itself [see Illustration 35]. Is it hard to revolve

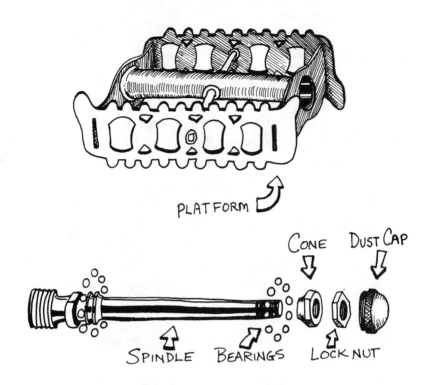

PLATFORM

CONE   DUST CAP

SPINDLE   BEARINGS   LOCK NUT

Illustration **35** PEDAL, EXPLODED VIEW

on its spindle by hand? Is it loose on the spindle? Is it obviously bent? When you spin it by hand, does it catch and grab? Have the dust cap and/or the locknut come off? For any of these symptoms, see *Pedal Problems.*

If you hear a *clunk* or sharp *squeak* each time you push down on one pedal or the other, or if you sometimes feel a slight *slippage of a pedal* as you push hard on it, or if one of your *cranks is knocking* on the frame or your kick stand each time it comes around, see *Cranks.*

If you hear grinding noises which you can't pin down on the pedals, or if your whole front half can slip back and forth or wiggle in the frame, or if the whole front half is hard to turn, then see *Bottom Bracket.*

Pedals

(cl) means clockwise, and usually tightens a nut or bolt. (c-cl) means counterclockwise, and usually loosens.

1, 3, 10. DESCRIPTION: What you push on with your feet to make the bike go. A pedal consists of a metal or metal and rubber platform, a spindle which is screwed into the crank, and bearing sets on which the platform revolves around the spindle. There is often a dust cap screwed or wedged onto the end of the spindle over the bearings. [See Illustration 35] There are also excellent sealed-bearing pedals, made by Phil Wood. They are costly, but will last a lifetime if you don't bang them around.

PROBLEMS: *Pedal loose or tight and noisy.* First make sure the spindle is screwed tightly into the crank. Tighten it if it isn't. Use a strong, flat, open-ended wrench on the flats you can see on the spindle right next to the crank. If you can't find a standard wrench that fits in there, buy a special pedal spanner from a shop or catalogue. The right pedal tightens *clockwise;* the left pedal tightens *counterclockwise.* [See Illustration 36]

If you have a dust cap over the outer end of the spindle, see if the cap has flat sides that you can put a big wrench or channel lock on. If there is some sort of wrenchable surface, unscrew (c-cl) the dust cap. If there are no wrenchable surfaces, pry the dust cap off with a screwdriver. Look inside. If you can wiggle the pedal back and forth on the spindle, back off (c-cl) the locknut on the end of the spindle, tighten (cl) the cone behind the locknut and back it off ¼ turn (c-cl), then tighten the locknut (cl). Put a drop of oil in there and try to get a drop into the bearings at the other end of the pedal too. If the pedal is tight (hard to turn), adjust

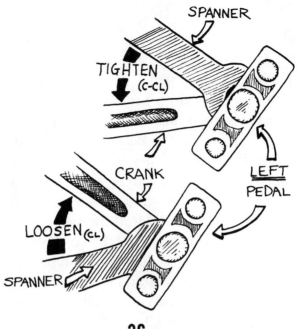

Illustration **36** PEDAL

the cone to make it looser (c-cl). As with all bearings, make the adjustment tight enough that there is no wiggle, but loose enough that the bearings turn freely without binding.

If you don't have a locknut and cone set-up under the dust cap, the pedal doesn't have ball bearings, and you can't adjust it. If you can possibly afford to, replace both pedals with ball bearing ones. Make sure you get ones that fit your crank. The best way to match a pedal is to take the bike and a wrench to the bike store, take the old pedal off there (remember, right pedal loosens c-cl, left pedal loosens cl), and get an *exact* replacement, checking it right there to make sure it fits in your crank. If the threads on the new pedal fit real tight or real loose in your crank (especially if the crank is aluminum), *don't* force the pedal on or try to tighten it in spite of its loose fit. The threads may be from different countries, and therefore cut at different angles; get a pedal with threads that match right, no matter how much of a hassle it is.

If adjusting the pedal bearings doesn't solve the problem, you can do a *pedal overhaul,* even though a pedal is never the same after it has made grinding and scraping noises. Put the pedal over a clean white rag. Take the dust cap off, if you haven't already, with a channel lock (or a screwdriver if it's the wedged-on kind). Back (c-cl) the locknut all the way off the spindle, and take the washer off. Hold the pedal on the spindle with one hand, and back (c-cl) the cone off the bearings. Count the bearings as they come. When they are all out of that end of the pedal, take the whole pedal platform off the spindle and count and catch the remaining bearings as they come. Clean all parts and replace any that are scored or dented. Are the bearing races in the platform scored? If they aren't, you can put grease in them and reconstruct the pedal. If they are, you might as well get a new pedal. Make sure it's the right size and fits your crank. Remember, the right pedal spindle loosens counterclockwise and the left loosens clockwise; you have to specify which side you are replacing when you buy a new one.

1, 3, 10. *Pedal bent, broken, or stripped off* so that you are left pushing on the spindle. Replace that pedal *now!* A spindle, or a weak, bent-up pedal is a dangerous thing. Take the bike and the correct wrench to a bike shop and get an exact replacement, testing the new pedal and spindle at the shop to make sure they fit onto your crank. Get a wrench that fits on the flats that are on the spindle right next to the crank; you may have to borrow or buy a special pedal spanner for the job. Remember, the right pedal loosens counterclockwise and the left pedal loosens clockwise. [See Illustration 36]

Cranks

(cl) means clockwise, and usually tightens a nut or bolt. (c-cl) means counterclockwise, and usually loosens.

1, 3, 10. DESCRIPTION: The cranks are the sturdy bars of solid metal which attach your pedals to the axle of the bottom bracket. The pedal is screwed into the crank. The crank is usually held to the bottom bracket axle by either a cotter pin or a bolt which goes through the crank and into the end of the axle; on many American bikes, the two cranks and the bottom bracket axle are all one solid piece of steel. The cranks, in order of mention, are called cottered cranks, cotterless cranks, and Ashtabula (such a beautiful name!) cranks. [See Illustration 37]

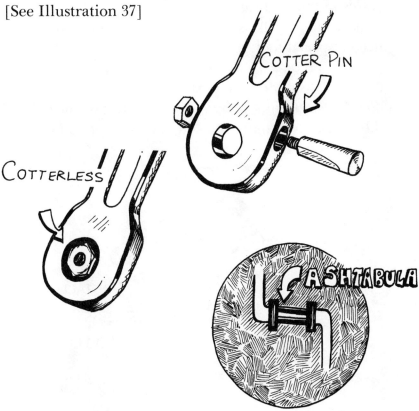

Illustration **37** CRANKS

PROBLEMS: *Clunk or sharp squeak* heard at each revolution of the pedal, or slight slippage felt, or both. Your *crank is loose* where it attaches to the bottom bracket axle. Don't ride the bike with a loose crank! Especially you cotterless crank people. To check to make sure that a loose crank is your problem, get off the bike and lean it against a wall, then put the pedals so they are level, one forward, and the other back. Get the weight of your body over the pedals. Push down sharply on both pedals at the same time with your hands. Feel anything give? Rotate the cranks 180 degrees and give the pedals another sharp push with your hands. Something give? Watch the joint of each crank and the axle as you push down in order to determine which crank is loose. To fix a loose crank, you need a special tool.

10. To fix a *loose cotterless crank,* buy a crank extractor and installer; it's inexpensive and easy to use. [See Illustration 38] Some of them are two-piece, like the illustrated tool, but others may be one-piece,

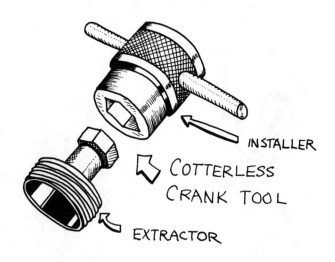

INSTALLER

COTTERLESS CRANK TOOL

EXTRACTOR

Illustration **38** COTTERLESS CRANK TOOL

requiring the use of a crescent or open-ended wrench. To tighten the loose crank, first unscrew (c-cl) the dust cap (if you have one) with the two-pronged gadget on the installer, or a big screwdriver if the cap has a slot. If the cap has a 5 mm Allen hex key hole in it, you have to use a hex key (Allen wrench). When the dust cap is off, take the socket of the installer and put it on the bolt that's in there. Tighten (cl) the bolt, shifting the crank back and forth on the axle as you do to make sure that it seats properly. Tighten up with a fair amount of torque on the bolt, but don't tighten it so hard that you destroy the bolt, or worse, the crank. If you have new cotterless cranks, repeat the tightening procedure once every 50 miles for the first 200 miles of use.

If a *cotterless crank won't stay tight,* no matter how tight the bolt is, try tightening the crank on the other side to make sure you've been working on the right one. No luck? The crank has a misshapen axle hole.

You have to *replace your cotterless crank.* If you are replacing a right crank, get the chain off the front sprocket and out of the way. First, remove (c-cl) the bolt with the installer. Then back (c-cl) the inner post of the extractor all the way out. Thread (cl) the whole extractor all the way into the dust cap threads. Put the socket of the installer or a socket wrench over the hex head of the extractor post. Screw in (cl) the extractor post until it pushes against the axle, loosening the crank. When the crank is good and loose, pull it straight off the end of the axle. Extract the extractor (c-cl) from the dust cap threads in the crank. If the threads in the crank get stripped in spite of all your precautions, go to a good machine shop and see if they can get it off with a gear puller. Take the old crank, and, if possible, the rest of the bike to a bike shop and get an exact replacement. They cost a lot. Don't be shocked.

To install a new crank, take the dust cap off (c-cl) if it has one. Clean and dry the crank and axle end meticulously, then smear some pipe thread compound, like Never-seez, on the flat surfaces at the end of the axle. Line the crank up so it's opposite the other one (unless you want to try a revolutionary pedaling cadence), and gently slip it onto the axle. Be careful! If you misshape the square hole in the soft metal of your new crank, it will never stay tight, and you will have wasted a lot of money replacing your old one. Get the bolt and washer, and start (cl) the bolt onto the axle with your fingers. When the bolt goes down inside the crank so you can't reach it with your fingers, put on the installer and screw in (cl) the bolt so it's snug. *Don't* tighten it yet. Shift the crank back and forth slightly on the axle when the bolt is snug, then tighten the bolt a bit at a time, making sure the crank is properly seated on the axle. Get the bolt good and tight. Screw in (cl) the dust cap and replace the chain on the sprocket if it's a right crank you replaced.

3, 10. *Loose cottered crank.* This is a tough one. You might think that all you need to do is tighten up on the cotter pin nut, but unfortunately, that won't wedge the pin tight enough [see Illustration 37]. You can either take a light hammer and tap the head of the pin (the opposite end from the nut), or you can take the bike to a shop where they can use a special tool with an enormous amount of leverage. If you try tapping the pin home, you are endangering your bottom bracket bearings. Any sharp blow on the pin will ram the ball bearings into their races, leaving a row of dents by a process called Brinelling. Brinelled bearings will slow you down and make nasty noises. So, if you can't find a shop with the right tool, you should use some sort of a holder-upper under the crank, so the taps of the hammer will travel down to the ground instead of into the bearings. To make a simple holder-upper, take a 9½ inch piece of ½ inch pipe that's threaded on one end and screw a floor flange onto that end. Stick it on the ground under the crank and tip the bike over so its weight is resting on the pipe, not the wheel, as in Illustration 38a. To find out if the pin is seated, tighten (cl) the nut on it, give the head of the pin another light tap, and see if you can tighten up any more on the nut. If you can, the pin isn't seated. Take your time, make sure you get the pin all the way home. But don't try to

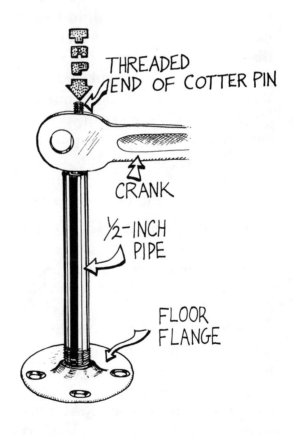

THREADED END OF COTTER PIN

CRANK

½-INCH PIPE

FLOOR FLANGE

Illustration **38a** TAPPING COTTER PIN

do that by tightening the cotter pin nut too tight; they tend to shear off. If you can't get it seated, see *Cottered crank replacement,* below.

Cottered crank replacement, though simple, requires caution and a holder-upper. First loosen the little locknut on the cotter (c-cl) until the top of the nut is flush with the end of the cotter. The end should be domed a little, and this dome should just barely stick up above the nut so you can hit it without hurting the nut or the cotter threads. Set the crank on the pipe holder-upper, as in Illustration 38a, but with the smooth end of the cotter down in the pipe and the nut end up where you can hit it. Use a light hammer and make *sure* you tap directly on the end of the cotter each time, so the force of the blow will go straight down the pin and through the crank and the pipe to the ground. When the pin comes loose, unscrew the nut (c-cl) the rest of the way, then take the pin out and take the crank and the pin with you for replacements, which must be *exact.* Put the new cotter pin in so it points down when the other one points up. The pins will *both* point either clockwise or counterclockwise around the axle.

1, 3, 10. *Crank knocking against frame of the bike.* Your crank is bent; it hits one of the chain stays each time it comes around. (If you have a 10 speed and your right crank is hitting the front changer cage, see *Front Changer.*) Repair requires a special lever that only bike shops have. Don't try to straighten the crank by hitting it with a hammer or prying it with a big crowbar; you'll just cause worse damage. Take the bike to a reputable shop and face the music, or do the appropriate *replacement* procedure above. Next time, be more careful about which pedal is down as you lean around a corner.

Bottom Bracket

(cl) means clockwise, and usually tightens a nut or bolt. (c-cl) means counterclockwise, and usually loosens.

1, 3, 10. DESCRIPTION: The bottom bracket is the part of the bike which holds the cranks in the frame and lets them spin freely. It consists of a heavy axle or spindle (on the Ashtabula set-up, the axle is just the middle portion of the one-piece crank), bearings, a fixed and an adjustable bearing cup, and a lockring for the adjustable bearing cup [see Illustration 39]. There are also great sealed-bearing bottom bracket sets, made for cotterless crank sets. My favorite is the bottom bracket set made by Phil Wood. It is tricky to install, and maybe worth leaving to someone who has done the job before, but once installed, this sealed-bearing set will last *forever,* with no adjustment, no lubrication, no nasty noises when you pedal!

PROBLEMS: *Bottom bracket loose or tight.* Either your whole axle is loose so that it can slide from side to side, or it is hard to turn the cranks at all. You have to adjust the adjustable bearing cup on the left side of the bottom bracket [see Illustration 39].

To adjust the bottom bracket of cottered or cotterless cranks: If you have a stamped metal spanner with a

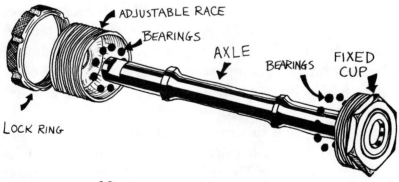

Illustration **39** BOTTOM BRACKET, EXPLODED VIEW

hook on it, use it to hook one of the notches in the lockring and loosen (c-cl) it. If necessary, use the light hammer lightly. If you don't have a spanner with one of those nifty hooks, use a screwdriver, set in one of the notches of the lockring at an angle, and a light hammer. Make sure you are loosening the lockring (c-cl). To adjust the adjustable bearing cup, take a small screwdriver and stick a corner of its blade in one of the little holes in the left end of the cup, then tap very lightly or push from an angle to move the cup the way it tightens. Tighten the cup, then back it off 1/8 turn. Tighten the lockring with the hooked spanner. Cranks still loose? Get a shop to check and tighten the fixed cup if needed.

1, 3, 10. For a *tight or loose Ashtabula crank,* adjust the left cone. Loosen (cl—that's backwards) the big locknut on the left side of the crank. Put a screwdriver in one of the slots on the left end of the cone (the thing under the locknut). To loosen the cone, turn it clockwise; to tighten the cone, turn it counterclockwise. If the cone is tightened (c-cl) against the bearings and then backed off (cl) 1/8 turn, it will be about right. Tighten up (c-cl) the big locknut when the cranks can turn smoothly without being loose.

If no amount of adjusting will get your bracket right, try a little oil. There are those who think bottom brackets should be oiled regularly. I think oil should be used only as a temporary remedy for bearing complaints. The bottom bracket bearings should be greased well once every year or so, and then left alone. The more oil there is floating around a bottom bracket, the more dirt is going to catch in it and eventually work its way into the works. For greasing, see Ashtabula *overhaul* below.

Nasty noises. When you pedal, grinding, or clanking, or grating noises occur that aren't attributable to the pedals. You need to *overhaul your bottom bracket.* Try adjusting it first, just to make sure. If you have cottered or cotterless cranks, see the *overhaul* procedure just below. If you have Ashtabula one-piece cranks, do the overhaul described on page 146.

10. For an *overhaul with cottered or cotterless cranks,* start by getting the cranks off. Remove them as described in *Cranks.* Put the bike upright in a rack or leaning against a wall, over a clean white rag. Get on the left side of the bike. Loosen (c-cl) the lockring on the adjustable cup. Stick either a hooked spanner or a screwdriver in one of the notches, and tap lightly with a light hammer. Unscrew the ring all the way and put it in a jar. Start loosening the adjustable cup by sticking needlenose pliers in the little holes in the end of the cup. When the cup is loose enough that the axle can slip back and forth, reach around to the right side of the bottom bracket and hold the axle tight against the fixed cup on that side. Now undo the adjustable cup with the other hand, working it out slowly, keeping the axle in place against the fixed cup as you go. When the adjustable cup comes free of the frame, pull it straight out over the end of the axle. Collect the bearings—not only the ones that stayed in the adjustable cup, but those nasty ones that stuck to the axle, or fell down inside the bottom bracket shell. Keep the axle held against the fixed cup. Don't turn the bike upside down —the bearings will just run down the frame tubes and hide where you can't get at them. Leave the bike right side up and get all the bearings out with your finger or a little magnet. Count them. Write the number here   . Put them all with the adjustable cup in the jar.

Pull the left end of the axle straight out of the bottom bracket. Catch all the bearings. Count them. Write it down here   . The number should be the same as for the other side. Lock the bearings up in the jar before they run away in search of heater vents or weed patches to hide in.

Look inside the empty bottom bracket shell, or hanger shell as some people call it. Is there a tube of thin plastic that fits around the axle in there? Take it out and save it with the other parts. It is an ingenious device for keeping grit that has gotten into the frame tubes from getting into the bottom bracket bearings and finishing them off. If it's all cracked and ruined, or not there at all, start a shopping list and put that at the top.

Clean out all the grit that has collected in the bottom bracket shell. Clean and look closely at the fixed cup. Use a flashlight if you can't see it well. Is it pitted? Is the shiny ring round, or nearly round? (It sometimes wears a little elliptical from the unbalanced pressure on the cranks, but the shiny place should be very close to round.) Unless the fixed cup is in bad shape, leave it alone. If it is really messed up, you can try to unscrew it (c-cl on most bikes, but *cl* on some English and Swiss bikes; watch out for that!) for replacement, but go easy, and don't hesitate to take the job to a shop if your tools are inadequate.

When you have all the parts of your bottom bracket (except the fixed bearing cup) in a jar, look at the bearing surfaces on the cups and the axle. Are the shiny rings out of round? Are there any pits or scored places? See Illustration 20a on page 74 if you need to get an idea of what shot bearings look like. Add to the shopping list as needed. Look at the balls themselves. Pitted? Scored? Add to the list, and get extras. Put grease on the list if you don't have some fine, light bike bearing grease like Lubriplate or Phil Wood. Take the parts that you need to replace to the bike shop. Make sure you get the right threads and sizes. Don't use any threaded replacement that is harder to get onto its threads than the old part was to get off. If the threads on the bottom bracket shell are ruined, you have to have the shop cut new threads.

To reconstruct your bottom bracket, lay the bike down on its right side and put grease around the race of the fixed cup. Stick the right number of ball bearings in the grease. (If the number you wrote down was right, i.e., enough that there were only small spaces between the bearings, put that number in.) Wipe off any extra grease. Extra grease attracts destructive grit to the bearings. Find the *long* end of the axle, and stick that end through the fixed cup. If you have a plastic tube, slip it into the bottom bracket shell around the axle. Block the frame up a little with a brick or something so the right end of the axle can stick down until the axle rests on the bearings. Hold the axle straight in place and spin it. Smooth? It feels so nice when it is. If it isn't, remove the axle and check for smoothness on all the bearing surfaces. If the axle turns smoothly on the fixed cup bearings, go on to the adjustable cup.

Put grease in the race of the adjustable cup and stick the right number of ball bearings in the grease. Remember, you want small gaps between the bearings. Put this prepared cup within arm's reach of where you're working on the bottom bracket. Now pick up the frame of the bike, holding the axle in place, and turn it over so the left end of the axle is off the floor. Now reach for that prepared adjustable cup, slide it under the left end of the axle, and screw it all the way up into the bottom bracket shell (cl). Tighten it with your fingers until the bearings seat on the axle. Now you can let go of the right end of the axle. Spin the lockring on; be careful as you start the threads—they are easy to strip. Hand tighten the adjustable cup until it is snug on the bearings, then back the cup off about 1/8 turn, and tighten the lockring, using the hooked spanner or a screwdriver and a light hammer. Tap lightly. Check for looseness or roughness of the axle. If it is just a bit rough, loosen the adjustable cup a bit, and see if you can get a smooth-running axle without getting a loose axle. If you can't, you have no choice but to take the works apart and track down the cause. Check again for grit and scoring on the surfaces. When you get a smooth and snug fitting axle, tighten up well on the lockring. Go to *Cranks* and replace your cranks. Put the chain back on the front sprocket, and you have finished.

1, 3, 10. If you have a *one-piece, or Ashtabula crank,* start the *bottom bracket overhaul* by unscrewing (clockwise, remember) the left pedal and taking the chain off the front sprocket. Then get a big wrench, like the Ford monkey wrench or a big crescent if you have one. The channel lock will do if you're careful. Get a good grip on the big locknut that's around the crank on the left side of the bottom bracket, hold the right crank with your other hand, and loosen (clockwise—that's backwards) that big nut. Put the big nut and the washer that should be under it in a jar. Unscrew (cl) the wide left bearing cone. It's the next thing screwed onto the bottom bracket axle. It has two slots in it. Start unscrewing it (cl) with a screwdriver in one of the slots if necessary. Hold the crank in place against the right set bearing cone. Don't worry about the ball bearings though. They are in retainers, and they won't jump out and run all over. That's so considerate. Good old Yankee ingenuity. Put the left bearing cone in the jar. Take out the ball bearings, leaving them in their retainer, and put them in the jar. Move the whole axle to the right, tipping it as you go, and thread the whole piece all the way out of the frame through the bottom bracket. Remove the ball bearings—still in their retainers—from the right side and put them in the jar. Look at all the bearing cups and cones. (The cups are set into the bottom bracket shell, and the right cone is screwed onto the axle.) If any of the bearing surfaces are pitted, or if the balls themselves are scored, or if any of the balls are missing, take the parts to a good bike shop and get exact replacements. If you need to get a cup out of the bottom bracket shell, stick the big screwdriver through the shell from the opposite side and tap around the rim of the cup to drive it out. [See Illustration 20 to get the idea] Using solvent and rags, thoroughly clean and dry the parts you don't replace.

To reconstruct a dismantled Ashtabula bottom bracket set, first screw (cl) the right cone (if you had to take it off) onto the crank. Squeeze bearing grease into the bearing retainers so that all the spaces around the balls are filled with grease. Wipe excess grease off the outside of the retainer rings and set them down on something *very clean* within arm's reach of your bottom bracket. Put one of the bearing rings onto the crank. Remember that the solid ring side of the retainer goes against the cone. If you put a new cup in the bottom bracket shell, make sure it is well seated. Tap around and around its edges to get it all the way in. Take the right crank in your right hand, and stick the left crank through the right end of the bottom bracket shell. It takes some tilting and angling around, but get that crank through without forcing anything. Now put the bearings over the left crank and follow them with the left cone. Remember, the left cone screws on counterclockwise. Tighten the left cone up on the bearings, then back off (cl) about 1/8 turn, or until the crank turns smoothly but doesn't wiggle. Put on the washer, then tighten up the big locknut. Get that nut good and tight, then check to make sure the cranks are still adjusted correctly. Put your left pedal back on (c-cl), get the chain back on the front sprocket, and you're set to go.

Front Sprocket (Chainwheel)

(cl) means clockwise, and usually tightens a nut or bolt. (c-cl) means counterclockwise, and usually loosens.

DESCRIPTION: The round metal wheel with all the points around it that pulls the chain when you pedal. On 1 or 3 speed bikes, the front sprocket is permanently attached to the right crank [see Illustration 40]. On 10 speed bikes, the crank has three or five arms, onto which the chainwheels are bolted. [See Illustration 41]

1, 3, 10. PROBLEMS: *Kerchunk* of chain each time it comes to one place on the sprocket. Get the bike up on a rack. Crank the pedals slowly and watch the chain as it goes onto the front sprocket. Does the chain kick up on one of the teeth of the sprocket each time that one tooth comes around? If so, you have a bent tooth. If the chain doesn't kick up on any one tooth, continue cranking slowly and watch the chain where it goes onto the rear sprocket, or in the case of a 10 speed, where it goes through the chain rollers on the changer. Does the chain kick up or jump a little back there every once in a while? Look closely at the chain where it jumps. Is a link of the chain tight? See *Chain Problems.* Is the

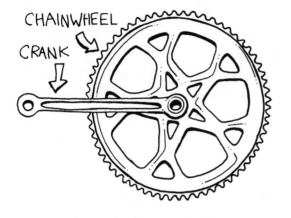

CHAINWHEEL

CRANK

Illustration **40**
PERMANENTLY
MOUNTED
CRANK
AND CHAINWHEEL

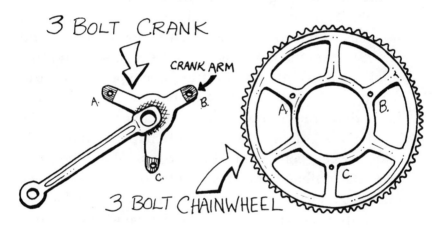

3 BOLT CRANK

CRANK ARM

A.   B.

C.

3 BOLT CHAINWHEEL

A.   B.

C.

Illustration **41** BOLT-TOGETHER CRANK AND CHAINWHEEL

chain kicking up each time it hits a particular tooth on the rear sprocket? See *Rear Sprocket Problems.*

If you have a *bent tooth on the front sprocket,* you have to play dentist. Mark the tooth that the chain kicked up on. Take the chain off the sprocket. On a 1 speed or 3 speed, if the chain is tight, you have to loosen (c-cl) the rear wheel axle nuts and slip the wheel forward to get the chain loose enough to slip the chain off the sprocket. [See *Wheel Removal*] With the chain off the front sprocket, spin the cranks slowly and look down from directly above the front sprocket. Watch closely for the marked tooth and the ones on either side of it. See the way the tooth is bent? If you can't see any bend in the tooth, look at it from the side. If it is chipped or worn down on one corner, you have to replace the sprocket [see *Changing the sprocket* below].

If your close examination of the tooth reveals that it is merely bent, put your crescent wrench on the bent tooth and tighten it up so that it grips the tooth firmly. Bend the tooth slightly. Take the crescent off and have a look. If the sprocket is steel, you will be amazed at how easily the tooth bends. If the sprocket is Dural alloy, like on the fancy racers' bikes, you will find that it takes a good bit more to straighten a bent tooth. But whichever type of sprocket you have, do your bending in moderation. You want to straighten one tooth, not bend the whole sprocket out of shape. If the whole sprocket gets bent, see below under *wobble.* When you have straightened your bent tooth, put the chain back on. On 1 and 3 speed bikes, pull the rear wheel back so the chain is nearly tight, then align the wheel between the stays and tighten the axle bolts [see *Wheel Replacement*]. Try the slow pedaling test. No more kerchunk? Good. If there is still a kerchunk, check the teeth and the chain again.

10. *The front sprocket has a wobble* in it, so that either one side of the chain or the other rubs against the changer cage at each revolution of the pedal. This is a tough one. Put the bike up on a rack. Crank the pedals slowly, and watch the chain where it goes past the changer cage. Find the area of the sprocket that is bent in or out so that the chain hits the changer cage. Mark the bent area of the sprocket. Sometimes it's hard

to tell whether the sprocket is bent in on one side or bent out on the other. Try to decide where the majority of the sprocket is, and call the rest bent in or bent out. Does the bent area that you marked correspond to one of the crank arms? Usually, a sprocket with a bad wobble is due to a bent crank arm or a bad connection between the arm and the sprocket [see Illustration 41]. Check all the bolts that hold the sprocket tight to the crank arms. They're all tight and you still have a wobble? The only way you can get that thing straight is with a hammer. Take a block of wood and put it against the sprocket where it is bolted to the crank arm (not the crank! See Illustration 41.) Give the wood block a good slug with the hammer. *Warning:* That slug can be destructive. The force of the blow will carry through the crank into the bottom bracket bearings and might do some damage there. Brinelling, it is called. The ball bearings drive right into the surface of their races. They leave a little row of dents so that when you pedal, the bearings have to run over a surface that's about as smooth as a washboard. So, if you are worried about Brinelling your bottom bracket bearings, keep the block in the same place on the chainwheel, but turn the cranks between each slug of your hammer on that block of wood.

Changing the sprocket on a 10 speed bike is easy. Unscrew (c-cl) the bolts that hold the sprocket to the crank, and save all the bolts, nuts, and washers [see Illustration 41]. Take the bad sprocket to a reliable bike shop and get a new sprocket that has exactly the same mounting holes. You don't have to get one with the same number of teeth, but remember, more teeth will be a higher gear, fewer teeth will be a lower gear. If you change to a larger big sprocket or a smaller little one, you may have to change the length of the chain, and that, in turn, may require a new freewheel and maybe a rear changer with a wider range. All in all, it's easier to keep the new sprockets the same sizes as the old ones. When you bolt on your new sprocket, make sure it's right side out, and tighten up (cl) the bolts a little at a time, working your way around and around the sprocket, so you don't bend the sprocket before you even get to use it.

1, 3. If you have a front sprocket that is permanently mounted on the crank [see Illustration 40], your crank will probably be cottered, so you will have to do the replacement with a cotter pin tool [see page 140]. If the front sprocket is a 1 speed or 3 speed Ashtabula crank, you have to remove and replace the whole crank [see *Bottom bracket overhaul*].

Chain

(cl) means clockwise, and usually tightens a nut or bolt. (c-cl) means counterclockwise, and usually loosens.

DESCRIPTION: The dirtiest part of the bike. It has rollers riveted to connecting plates and connects the front and rear sprockets [see Illustration 42]. There are several different standard sizes, none of which are interchangeable. On most 1 and 3 speed bikes, one link,

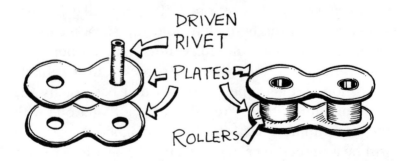

Illustration **42** TWO CHAIN LINKS

Illustration **43** MASTER LINK

the master link, has a U-shaped or oversized plate on one side that can be popped on and off. [See Illustration 43] Ten speed bikes do not have master links.

1, 3, 10. PROBLEMS: You have a *thrown chain,* which means your chain has come off one or more of the sprockets, and now you want to put it back. (Ten speed people: the most common cause of a thrown chain is a changer in need of adjustment — see *Changers, General.*) Put the chain on the rear sprocket first. If you have a 10 speed, you have to thread the chain through the tension roller, the jockey roller, and over the smallest rear sprocket [see Illustration 33], and make sure you have your gear lever in high gear position. Everybody, with the back part of the chain the way it's supposed to be, press a couple of chain links down over the teeth at the top of the front sprocket. Crank the pedals forward while holding those links on the sprocket teeth, and the rest of the chain will pop onto the sprocket. If you can't figure out why your chain came off, it could be any one of the *Problems* described in this *Chain* section.

1, 3, 10. *Squeaky or gunk-covered chain.* You haven't oiled or cleaned it in a while. It's easy to forget. But it's one of the few maintenance items that must be kept up with. Before you oil the chain, see how dirty it is. Depending on how bad it is, you might take some solvent on a rag and rub it down, cranking the pedals to move the chain through the rag, or if it's shot you might even replace it [see *Chain replacement*]. If the chain is very dirty but not shot, take it off as in *Chain replacement,* then soak it in solvent and wipe it clean and replace it as if it were a new chain.

To oil the chain, get a can of light (ten to thirty weight) oil with a thin spout and hold it upside-down over the front of the front sprocket so that the oil will drip down onto the chain at its frontmost point. If you have a 3 or 10 speed, crank the pedals backwards slowly as you let the oil go from roller to roller of the chain. If you have a 1 speed, foot brake bike, you can't pedal backwards. Get the bike up on a rack and pedal forwards as you let the oil go from roller to roller of the chain. Go easy on the oil whichever kind of bike you are working on. It only takes a small drop on each roller all the way around. When you have put that much oil on the chain, take an old rag and squirt a little oil on it. Spread the oil around on the rag, then hold the oily rag around the part of the chain that's stretched between the bottom of the front and rear sprockets. Rotate the cranks back and forth to spread an even, thin film of oil all over the chain. You don't want lots of extra oil on your chain. It attracts grit, which will raise the friction coefficient higher than the oil can lower it. Especially if you ride near the beach where any extra oil picks up stray sand. Go for a ride on your bike with a newly oiled chain. Incredible difference, isn't there? Remember that. Keep the chain covered with a thin coat of light oil. Check it every month in dry weather, every two weeks during the rainy season.

1, 3, 10. You have a *loose chain.* Your chain sags down between the front and rear sprockets. To tighten the chain on 1 or 3 speed bikes, loosen the big axle nuts that hold the rear wheel to the frame. Pull the rear wheel back in the frame. When the chain is tight enough so you can grab a point of the chain halfway between the sprockets and move it up and down only about ½ inch, tighten the right axle nut. Align the wheel so the rim is in the middle of the chainstays, and tighten the left big axle nut (if you need help, see *Wheel Removal* and *Wheel Replacement*).

10. The chain is loose on a 10 speed bike if the rear changer can't take up all the slack chain when the front and rear changers are both in small sprocket positions. Shift both the changers to the large sprocket positions. Is the chain still loose? If, when the chain is on the biggest sprockets, it isn't so tight that it pulls the rear changer forward to a horizontal position, you can take a link out of the chain with the chain tool, and connect the ends of the chain back together as in *Chain replacement*. If removing a link doesn't help tighten up the chain, you probably have a weak or broken pivot bolt spring in your rear changer. [See *Rear Changer overhaul*]

1, 3, 10. *Tight link.* When one part of the chain goes over a sprocket, especially a small rear sprocket, the chain kinks. When the same part of the chain comes off the sprocket, it doesn't come completely unkinked. If you suspect that you have a tight link, get the bike up on a rack and crank the pedals slowly. Watch the chain as it goes over the rear sprocket, or, in the case of a 10 speed, through the chain rollers [see Illustration 32]. Does the chain jump a little each time one link comes around? That's your tight link. You can find the one for sure by flexing the jumpy area of the chain with your fingers until you find the one that doesn't want to flex. When you have found the tight link, mark it.

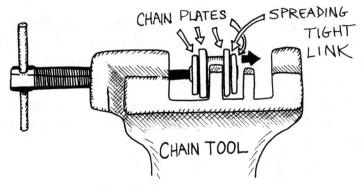

Illustration **44 a**   USING A CHAIN TOOL

Before doing anything drastic, try some fine oil on the tight link. Work the oil in by flexing the link with your fingers, not only up and down, but from side to side, so you can loosen up the rivets in the side-plates, and make more room between them for the rollers. No luck? Get your chain tool and turn (c-cl) the handle so the point moves back almost out of sight. Put the rivet of the tight link in the spreader slot (the slot nearest the twisting handle—see Illustration 44a). Screw (cl) the point of the chain tool until it hits the end of the rivet. Make sure you have the chain straight in the slot, and the point of the tool butted up against the end of the tight rivet. Turn the handle of the chain tool ¼ turn. No more. Back (c-cl) the point of the tool off the rivet and take the chain out of the spreader slot. Is the link looser? Try some oil. Still tight? Try another ¼ turn with the chain tool. Check to make sure the side plates of that link aren't bent. If they are, see *Chain replacement.* If the link is no longer tight, look closely at the rivet that you just loosened. Is there more of it sticking out on one end than the other? It's not serious if the difference is very slight, especially on a 1 or 3 speed bike. On a 10 speed bike, both ends of the chain rivet should be very close to equal. On no bike should either

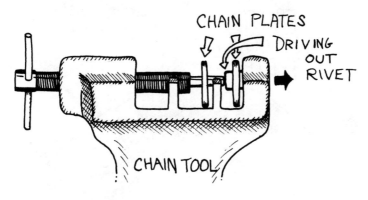

CHAIN PLATES

DRIVING OUT RIVET

CHAIN TOOL

Illustration **44 b**   USING A CHAIN TOOL

end of a rivet be driven in until it is flush with the side plate of the chain. Drive the rivet from the other side of the chain to even things up [see Illustration 44b]. Test the chain while the bike is still on the rack. Often, a chain that has one tight link will have others that are almost tight. Oil the chain [see *Squeaky chain*].

1, 3, 10. *Chain worn out, ready for replacement,* or lots of *kerchunking.* Your chain has seen a lot of service, or has been damaged by mistreatment. The chain has a lifespan. You can't expect it to survive more than three years of normal usage, or two years of heavy usage. So when your chain starts kerchunking a lot, and you can't find any bad sprocket teeth or tight links to blame the trouble on, test the chain to see if it is ready for retirement. First check the deflection of the chain by moving it from side to side. It should not be so worn that it can deflect more than an inch, even if it is loose on the sprockets.

If there is a lot of side-to-side deflection, grab a link of the chain that is on the front sprocket and pull it forward, as in Illustration 44c. If the link slacks out as far as the chain in the illustration, then the thing is over the hill. You have to *replace* the old chain.

On 1 and 3 speed bikes, find a U-shaped or wide

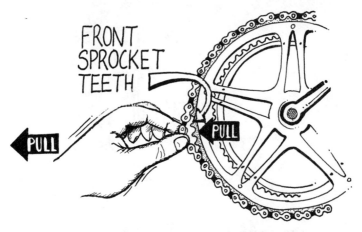

FRONT SPROCKET TEETH

PULL

PULL

Illustration 44c   CHECKING CHAIN LOOSENESS

plate on one of the links (called the master link). Pry that plate off [see Illustration 43]. On 10 speed bikes, take the chain tool and put a link in the driving slot (the one farthest from the twist handle—see Illustration 44b). Screw (cl) the driving point in until it hits one of the chain rivets. Make sure the point is butted up square on the end of the rivet. Drive (cl) the rivet out until the end that's *farthest* from the driving point is just flush with the outer edge of the casing of the chain tool, then *stop!* Don't drive the rivet all the way out of the chain [see Illustration 42]. Back (c-cl) the point of the chain tool all the way out of the hole in the chain. Take the chain out of the slot in the tool. Does the chain come apart? If not, hold the chain on either side of the driven-out rivet. The rivet is pointing away from you. Now bend both sides of the chain towards you so that the plates spread a bit and release the driven-out rivet. Don't bend the chain hard—you'll just misshape the plates. Take the chain off the bike; go to a good shop and get as high quality an exact replacement as you can afford.

For 10 speeds you have to get a longer chain and shorten it to the number of links of your old chain.

One end of the new chain will be the narrow link with the roller between the ends of the plates. The other end will have two widely spaced plates with no roller between them [see Illustration 42]. Remove the extra links of chain from the end with the widely spaced plates with no roller between them. Drive out the rivet of a link that will create a matching end. Put the chain on the bike, stick the two ends of the chain together, and drive the rivet home (until equal ends stick out the side plates) to complete the new chain. Make sure you have the chain on the bike correctly before you drive in the connecting rivet.

If you have to drive a new rivet to replace your chain, check the link that you have just riveted. It often gets tightened up in the rivet-driving process. To loosen it, see *Tight link* above. On a 10 speed, if you replace your chain, you often have to replace the rear sprockets. They wear down, and a new chain won't fit them. See *Rear Sprocket Problems.*

1, 3. On 1 and 3 speed bikes, it's a lot easier to put the new chain together if you loosen the rear axle nuts and slip the rear wheel forward a bit. Put the chain around the front and rear sprockets and pinch the master link on with pliers. Pull the wheel back in the drop-outs so the chain is tight, then realign the wheel, and tighten the big nuts.

Back Half, General

(cl) means clockwise, and usually tightens a nut or bolt. (c-cl) means counterclockwise, and usually loosens.

DESCRIPTION: The rear half of the power train consists of the rear sprocket or sprockets (which on 10 speeds are mounted as a cluster on a freewheel) and the rear gear changer.

Rear Sprocket

1, 3, 10. DESCRIPTION: The little metal wheel with the points on it for the chain, which is attached to the right side of the rear wheel. For 1 and 3 speed people, this part is so obvious and trouble-free that I hardly need mention it. For 10 speed people, however, there are five rear sprockets, all attached as a cluster to a freewheel which has a ratchet and is screwed onto the hub of the wheel. That freewheel ratchet is the reason the bike doesn't go backwards when you pedal backwards; it also lets you stop pedaling while riding forward. The sprockets on the freewheel vary widely in size, and therefore in number of teeth. The larger a rear sprocket is, the more teeth it has, and the lower it makes the gear. The front sprockets are just the reverse. Say to yourself a few times, "Front larger higher, rear larger lower," to get it memorized.

PROBLEMS: *Kerchunk.* Your chain kicks up about twice to every revolution of the pedals. Check first to make sure the kerchunk isn't due to a faulty chain or front sprocket. If a 1 or 3 speed rear sprocket is causing the kerchunk, remove the wheel [see *Wheel Removal*] and have a shop replace the sprocket. If it's a 10 speed, get the bike up on a rack and rotate the pedals slowly. Look closely at the teeth of the sprockets. The gap between each tooth should be a perfectly regular U shape. If the top corners of the teeth are all rounded off, or if one side of the gap between the teeth is worn in at all, then the freewheel needs replacing.

10. *Freewheel removal and replacement.* Get the bike up on a rack and remove the rear wheel [see *Wheel Removal*]. Unscrew (c-cl) the big axle nut or wingnut or quick-release conical nut off the right end of the axle. (If you have a quick-release, a spring will come off

the axle—don't lose it.) Put whichever you have in a jar where you won't lose it. See if your freewheel remover will fit into place on the freewheel around the axle. If it won't, the spacer nut on the axle is in the way. Get a thin spanner and put it on the *left* cone. Get another spanner or a wrench on the spacer nut (the end of the spacer nut is hex-shaped, just like a thin locknut), loosen (c-cl) it, and unscrew it all the way off the axle. Put it in the jar.

Now put the remover in place so that either the splines are well engaged, or the two prongs are set *all* the way down in their slots on the freewheel. [See Illustration 45]. Put the big axle nut, or the conical quick-release nut (without its spring) back on the axle and screw (c-cl) it up to the freewheel remover. Take a big wrench and get a good grip on the remover. To loosen the freewheel, you have to turn it counterclockwise. Getting the freewheel loose is often very difficult, especially if the wheel and freewheel have been together for a long time or you are a strong rider. Make sure you are turning the remover correctly (c-cl). Also

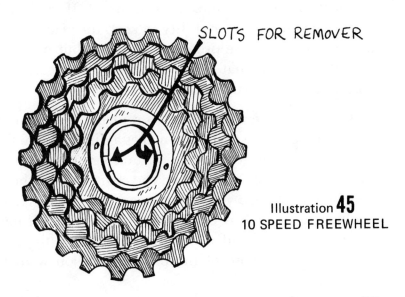

SLOTS FOR REMOVER

Illustration **45**
10 SPEED FREEWHEEL

make sure that the big axle nut or the quick-release conical nut is holding the remover snug against the freewheel. Turn the wrench gradually harder and harder. If you feel something give, check to make sure the freewheel is coming loose and not stripping. (Often, with the pronged remover, the "give" is from the remover gouging into the freewheel.) If the freewheel comes loose, loosen the big axle nut (cl) or the quick-release conical nut and spin (c-cl) the freewheel off the hub. If the freewheel starts to strip, don't try to get it off—you'll just strip it more. Take off the remover and take the wheel to a shop. They will hopefully be able to get the thing off.

When you have spun the freewheel all the way off, you may find one or two little spacer rings underneath it. Save these and put them under the new freewheel. You may have a big wide metal or plastic plate under the freewheel, too. This is a spoke protector, which is meant to keep the chain from running into the spokes if your derailleur gets out of adjustment. I think you should throw this dead-weight item away and promise yourself to keep the derailleur adjusted. If you don't trust yourself and your ability to keep the gears tuned up, you can keep the protector on there, but it's a sad sort of statement that you don't even trust *yourself* to take care of your trusty bike.

Get a good new freewheel to replace your old one if you can. Splurge a little. It makes a difference in the smoothness of the gear operation, and a good freewheel will last longer, too. Whenever you change a freewheel, you have to change your chain, especially if the chain is old. Old, stretched chains tend to kick up on new sprockets. You should match the sprockets of the new freewheel with those of the old one. If you want to change to a freewheel with a bigger large rear sprocket, you will have to get more chain. This, in turn, will often tax the tension roller on your changer beyond its capabilities. You will have to change the entire changer system, just to get a slightly lower gear. You should also think twice about getting a very small (13 tooth) sprocket for the high gear. These work only with a super-strong chain, and even then, they tend to make the chain kick up. They also wear out faster than 14 tooth sprockets.

Put some Never-seez or similar thread compound on the threads of the new freewheel, then hold the freewheel in one hand, and the wheel (with the spacers on it) in the other, and get ready to start threading the freewheel on. *Careful.* The aluminum alloy used for many hubs is soft. To make sure you get a good start, hold the center section of the freewheel against the axle with a finger and twist counterclockwise, keeping the freewheel exactly vertical, until you feel the threads join. Then twist gently clockwise. Stop immediately if there is any resistance, back the freewheel off (c-cl), using the remover if necessary, and try again. Persevere. When the freewheel finally spins on, it's gratifying. You don't have to tighten up the freewheel. You will do that automatically as you pedal. Put the spacer back on the axle if you had it off, and the big axle nut or the quick-release conical nut and its spring. Put the wheel back in the frame, hook up your new chain [see *Chain Replacement*], and you're set to go. After you've ridden the bike a little, and tightened the freewheel on well by pedaling, check the rear changer adjustment, as described on page 184.

Changers, General

(cl) means clockwise, and usually tightens a nut or bolt.
(c-cl) means counterclockwise, and usually loosens.

3, 10. DESCRIPTION: The changers are the devices for shifting the gears on a bicycle.

One type of changer shifts cogged planet gears in a hub. This type of changer is most common on 3 speed models, but lately a 5 speed innovation has begun to appear. The planet gear changer, when well built, is definitely the most reliable changer there is. The system requires only oiling and adjustment of the indicator chain. However, the 3 speed hub has a limited range and the planet gear power transmission is relatively poor. A lot of a rider's energy dissipates in the works of a 3 speed planet gear hub. Also, when the hub finally does wear down or when some part of it breaks, repair is an extremely complicated matter—much too complicated to be covered in this book.

The other kind of changer is the derailleur type, which moves the chain from larger to smaller sprockets, thus increasing or decreasing the gear ratio. This type of system offers a wider range of gears, transmits much more of a rider's energy to the rear wheel, and is comparatively easy to repair because of its accessibility. But it also requires a great deal more attention and caution than the hub system, and it is more fragile because of its unprotected location.

Hub Changer

(cl) means clockwise, and usually tightens a nut or bolt.
(c-cl) means counterclockwise, and usually loosens.

3. DESCRIPTION: This system consists of a control lever, which is usually mounted on the handlebars, a cable that is partially housed, an indicator chain, which

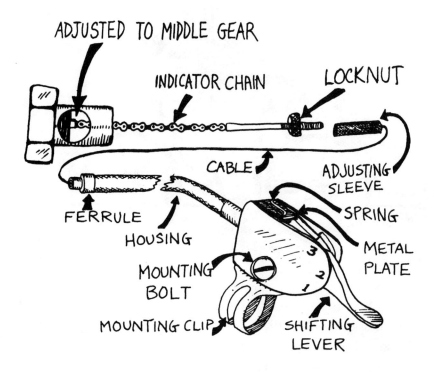

ADJUSTED TO MIDDLE GEAR

INDICATOR CHAIN

LOCKNUT

CABLE

ADJUSTING SLEEVE

FERRULE

HOUSING

SPRING

METAL PLATE

MOUNTING BOLT

MOUNTING CLIP

SHIFTING LEVER

Illustration **34** 3 SPEED GEARS
(repeated)

is adjustable, and a mechanism in the hub of the rear wheel. When problems occur, always remember that they might be due to trouble in any or all of the three units—control lever, cable, or mechanism.

3. PROBLEMS: *Gear slippage or loss.* Your middle gear, the one with the "N" on the control lever, suddenly changes from "N" for Normal to "N" for Neutral. Your feet fall off the pedals, and you make a painful landing on the top tube of the bike, or if it's a girl's bike, the down tube. Ouch. You may discover your *slippage* in a less painful way. Often the control lever can't get the hub into the low or middle gear at all.

The cause of gear slippage, in 99 cases out of 100, is improper lubrication and adjustment. (In the 100th case, when slippage cannot be corrected by oiling and adjusting, take the wheel out as in *Wheel Removal,* and take it to a good shop for overhaul.)

To oil the 3 speed hub, find the lubricating nipple on the hub casing and squirt in about three healthy slugs of fine, light oil like Sturmey Archer or Automatic Transmission Fluid (the pink stuff). Put a drop or two in the control lever too.

To adjust the hub, put the bike up on a rack and put it in high gear. Make sure that the hub, not just the control lever, is in high gear. Loosen (cl) the knurled locknut on the indicator. Tighten (cl) the sleeve by hand until there is only a little slack in the cable. Lock (c-cl) the locknut up against the sleeve. Get the control lever into the "N" or middle gear. Look closely at the indicator through the hole on the side of the long pole-shaped nut that the indicator goes through. In that hole, you should be able to see the end of the axle. If the indicator is in the middle gear position, the shoulder of the smooth pole that goes into the middle of the hub [see Illustration 34] should be just visible, sticking out of the end of the axle. Adjust the sleeve on the indicator if necessary. Tighten the locknut. Still getting slippage? Make sure the metal band that holds the cable fulcrum ferrule [see Illustration 34] is cinched tight around the frame. If it slips, the gears slip. If it's solid, maybe the indicator is messed up, or not screwed in all the way. Put the lever to the high gear. Remove (c-cl) the sleeve from the indicator completely. Try screwing (cl) the indicator into the hub farther. Don't get rough with it—it's delicate. Just tighten it by hand. But try to get it screwed in until it's snug. If you have to back it off (c-cl) a half turn or less to get the chain going at an angle that allows flex, that's OK, but don't loosen it any more than that. If the indicator is rusty or all mashed and bent, take it out (c-cl) and go to a bike shop for a new one that's the same size. Get a spare while you're at it. Put in (cl) the new indicator, making sure that you get it all the way in until it is snug. Put the sleeve on and tighten (cl) it until there is only a little slack in high gear. Tighten up (c-cl) the locknut. Shift the lever to the middle gear and check the adjustment at the end of the axle. Get it right. Make sure you tighten (c-cl) the locknut well (but without using any tools that will mash it) when you are finished. Ride in peace. You won't be hitting that top tube for a while.

3. *Cable broken.* First look at the whole cable and control lever set-up. Is everything pretty old and grungy? Is the lever messed up so that it slips all the time? Consider getting a new handlebar control lever [see Illustration 34], especially if your messed-up one is one of those in the hand grip, or one of those plastic monsters on the top tube. Get a standard handle-bar mounted hand lever. They're more reliable. To get an

old cable off a bike, you have to remove the big clamp that holds the fulcrum ferrule to the frame of the bike. Loosen (c-cl) the screw that holds on the clamp. Get the end of the housing, and the ferrule (the little plastic or metal sleeve) that holds it, out of the clamp. If you are sure your control lever is OK, get the end of the cable out of it. For ball bearing lever (or hand grip) people, unscrew (c-cl) the screws that hold the casing of the control lever together, and catch the ball bearing and its little washer as they fall out. Take the end of the cable out of its slot. Look at the race that the little bearing was running in from pocket to pocket for the different gears. If that race is worn into the metal, replace the whole lever with one of the standard handlebar-mounted control levers.

To get the cable out of a standard lever, pry up the little flat piece of metal with a wire spring on it that is at the top of the control lever [see Illustration 34]. Push the cable from the outside of the control lever, so the end comes up out of its slot, then pull the cable end back under the little flat piece that you pried up and out of the control lever. Take the pieces of the old broken cable and the housing to a bike shop. Get a new cable and housing that are the same length as your old one, and get a new control lever if you can find any excuse to; they can save you from so much pain. Get a new ferrule for the end of the housing if your old one was beat up or decayed with age. Put the ferrule around the end of your new housing and push the indicator sleeve through the hole in the clamp that holds the ferrule. Then push the ferrule into the clamp. To put the end of the cable in the new control lever, pry up the little piece of metal with the spring over it in the control lever [see Illustration 34], and push the end of the cable through until it sticks out from under the little flat piece. Put the control into the high gear position and slip the end of the cable down into its slot.

Thread the other end of the cable over its roller, and screw (cl) the sleeve onto the indicator. If the cable is too long or too short, you can adjust it to roughly the right length by moving the big clamp that holds the housing end ferrule up and down the frame. When you get them right, make sure the ferrule is holding the end of the housing so that it is seated. If no amount of adjusting the clamp will get your cable short enough, you can try to get another cable that's shorter, or you can get a cable with an adjustable sleeve. It has a little cable anchor bolt on it that you can tighten up anywhere on the cable. Just make sure you get it *tight* on the cable, so there's no chance of it slipping a bit and causing you to hit that top tube when the gears go into neutral. Adjust the cable as in the procedure in *Cable slippage* above.

Derailleur Type
Changers, General

(cl) means clockwise, and usually tightens a nut or bolt.
(c-cl) means counterclockwise, and usually loosens.

10. DESCRIPTION AND DIAGNOSIS:
Derailleur type changer systems are made up of a control lever unit, a cable, and a changer mechanism. The front and rear changers are quite different in design and function, but the control levers and cables are structurally identical. If you have *gear slippage,* particularly a tendency of the chain to slip from a large sprocket to a smaller sprocket, either front or rear, check the control lever first, then the cable, before you tackle the changer mechanism.

If your *chain is throwing,* find out which sprocket, front or rear, it throws off first, then see *Front Changer*

Mechanism Problems or *Rear Changer Mechanism Problems.* Two hints that will save you from many changer problems: *Don't ever lay a 10 speed bike down on its right side, and don't backpedal a 10 speed as you shift!*

If your *chain rubs or makes grindy noises* as you pedal, first fiddle with the lever for the front changer; if that doesn't get rid of the noise, see if the chain is rubbing against the sides of the front changer. If it is, and your lever-fiddling doesn't help, see *rubbing* on page 177. If the grindy noises *still* go on after that, and your chain is oiled, the problem may come from sprockets that are bent or out of alignment [see *sprocket alignment,* page 181]. If all of those things check out and you still have grindy noises, maybe you are simply using a combination of sprockets that your bike isn't up to using. On some 10 speed bikes, it isn't possible for the chain to run from the biggest front sprocket to the biggest rear sprocket; on others, it can't run from the littlest front sprocket to the littlest rear one. The chain runs at too sharp an angle; it is either stretched too tight or sagging too loose in these positions. It's a real strain on the system, and it tells you this by grinding and rubbing.

If this is the case with your bike, just avoid using those extreme combinations; the gears can be matched with other combinations. For instance, the gear you get by using the smallest front and back sprockets will be matched, roughly, by using the big sprocket in front and the second to smallest sprocket in back. Surprise! Your 10 speed is really an 8 speed.

Control Lever

10. DESCRIPTION: There are two basically different types, and several different models of each type.

There is a down tube type, which is usually attached

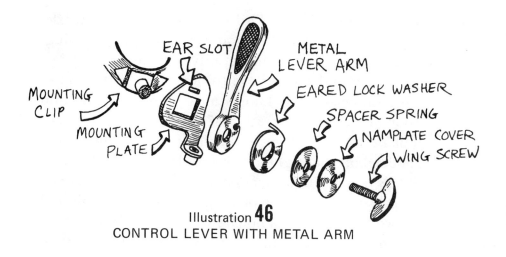

Illustration **46**
CONTROL LEVER WITH METAL ARM

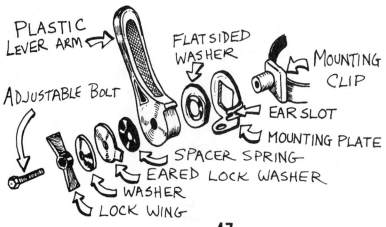

Illustration **47**
CONTROL LEVER WITH PLASTIC ARM

by a clamp to the down tube of the bike frame, but which may be attached to the stem. People call this model a "stem shifter" but it is really just a down tube type that has been moved up to the stem for a very dubious notion of convenience. All down tube shifters have a long lever that is held in place by a wing screw, a plastic wing on a bolt, a little wire wing screw, or a Phillips screw. All of these things can be adjusted (except for the nasty Phillips screw) while you ride. If your gears slip a little, you just tighten up the wing-thing a bit, and continue happily on your way.

The second type of control lever fits in the end of the handlebar. It is known as a tip shifter; the Sun Tour brand, in Illustration 47a, is common and very reliable for the price. It is held in the bar by an expander bolt that tightens *c-cl* and loosens *cl*. The head of this bolt is hidden under the lever, though, so you have to take the lever off to get at it. Take a big old screwdriver and file a notch in the end, as shown, then loosen (c-cl) and remove the slotted nut first, then unscrew (c-cl) the pivot bolt. When reassembling, slide the lever in so the square bump fits into the square slot, then put the hex-nut in its hex-hole and screw the pivot bolt in (cl) until it is snug. This adjustable pivot bolt also serves as the tension bolt, like the wing bolt on the other levers. Tighten it (cl) until the lever works

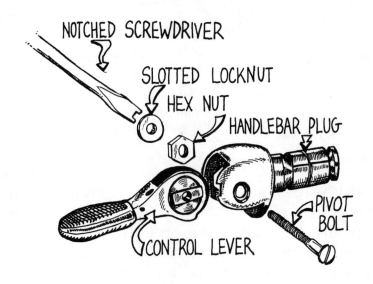

Illustration **47a**   TIP SHIFTER

smoothly but with resistance, then tighten the slotted nut (cl) with the notched screwdriver.

PROBLEMS: *Slippage* or stickies. Either your lever is very easy to move back and forth, and moves by itself, allowing the gears to shift, or your lever is hard to move, and then moves by itself after you shift. *Don't* oil the control lever. Usually, the problem with a slipping or sticky control lever is the adjustment of the wing bolt or screw. If the lever is slipping, tighten (cl) the wing bolt. If the lever is so tight that you have trouble shifting smoothly, loosen (c-cl) the wing bolt a bit. You tip shifter people, loosen the slotted locknut, then tighten the pivot bolt, as above. If the stickiness persists, you may have a dirty unit. To clean it, you have to take it apart by unscrewing (c-cl) the adjustable bolt. Watch it! There are quite a few little hard-to-distinguish parts held together by that bolt. As the bolt comes out, try to hold things together with your fingers and take them apart one piece at a time, memorizing the order of things as you go. The samples I have illustrated are common, but there are many variations. Get the order of your parts straight. If parts spew all over when you take the adjustable bolt off, look at an identical lever, like the other one on your bike if you have two. Clean all the rubbing surfaces with a clean dry rag. Use fine steel wool on the metal parts if you have to. If any of the parts is badly rusted or bent, take it to a good shop and get an exact replacement. When reconstructing things, check again to make *sure* they are in the right order. Also, make sure the washer with an ear or "dog" on it goes on so the ear fits in its slot [see Illustrations 46 and 47]. Tighten (cl) or loosen (c-cl) the bolt so that the lever can turn smoothly, but not loosely. Are you still getting slippage? Go on to the cable section.

Cable

(cl) means clockwise, and usually tightens a nut or bolt.
(c-cl) means counterclockwise, and usually loosens.

10. DESCRIPTION: A thin cable (thinner than a brake cable) that runs unhoused from a ball, cylinder, or small barrel end in the control lever down to the bottom bracket, where it makes a curve through a metal guide or a length of housing. From the bottom bracket, the rear changer cable runs unhoused to a cable stop near the rear end of the chain stay, then through housing to the rear changer mechanism, where it is held in an anchor bolt. The front changer cable runs from the bottom bracket curve directly to the anchor bolt on the front changer mechanism. If you have tip or stem shifters, there will be some housing around the cable, between the lever and a housing stop that is bolted onto the down tube of the frame.

PROBLEMS: *Stickies.* When you shift your control lever, the gears do not change immediately, but wait a while, then shift when you least expect them to. Or they slip just enough that the chain gets hung up between two sprockets and spins wildly around and around. Put the lever all the way forward. Look closely at the cable where it comes out of the control lever unit, and where it goes into and comes out of any housing. Is the cable frayed anywhere? Replace it if it's frayed at all. Gear cables have to take an amazing amount of strain.

To replace a frayed or broken cable, loosen the anchor bolt on the mechanism and pull the cable out of the housing and the control lever. Get a new cable with the same sort of control lever end.

When you get a new cable, don't cut it to size until you have threaded it through the housing and the cable anchor bolt. When the cable is threaded, push the control lever all the way forward. If you are working on a front changer cable, move the mechanism to the lowest gear position. You may have a real oddball front derailleur that won't stay in low, but rather goes to high by itself; if so, just attach the cable with the fershlugginger thing in high gear. If it's a rear changer cable, move the mechanism (or let it spring itself) to the highest gear position. Tighten (cl) the anchor bolt. Try the gears out, and adjust the adjustable bolt on the control lever or changer (see *Changer Mechanism* if necessary).

If your cable is not broken or frayed, but you find grit, rust, and gunk at the housing ends, or a kink in the housing, loosen the cable anchor bolt on the mechanism as if you were going to remove the cable. Pull on the mechanism end of the cable with one hand, and operate the control lever with the other. Try oil on the housing ends. For a rear changer cable, try holding the mechanism end of the cable with one hand and pulling the open section of cable that runs along the chain stay with the other. Is there stickiness in the rear section of the cable housing? If not, test for stickies in the front section of housing if there is one. When you find the area of stickiness, check the housing for kinks, grit clogging it up, or burrs in the ends, and check the cable for evidence of wear. Buy new housing and cable as needed. Cut the housing to match the length of the old pieces *exactly*. When cutting the housing, work the blades of the wire clipper between the coils, then twist as you cut the wire coil off clean. Check for burrs at the ends of the pieces of housing. Any burr pointing out into the air you can file off. But if there are inner burrs, recut the cable [see Illustration 6]. The front section of housing, where the cable curves at the bottom bracket, is a common place for grit to gather. If you have a housing there, and a lot of trouble with grit, you can buy a curved metal sleeve with a bracket that goes around the down tube. This set-up will replace the housing, and collect less grit. If the cable binds as it goes through the short piece of housing that passes over the axle of the rear wheel, it may be because this piece of housing is too short or too long. Cut a new piece of housing that can just make the short arch needed to get around the axle without binding on it.

Changer Mechanism, General

10. DESCRIPTION: The thing that moves the chain from sprocket to sprocket. The front and rear changers are very different in construction and function, and there are several significantly different models of each changer. The front changer is essentially no more than two metal fingers (the sides of the cage) which push the chain from sprocket to sprocket. The rear changer has two rollers through which the chain passes, instead of two metal fingers. The rollers not only guide the chain from sprocket to sprocket — they also take up the slack chain with a spring action when the chain is on a small sprocket.

Front Changer

(cl) means clockwise, and usually tightens a nut or bolt. (c-cl) means counterclockwise, and usually loosens.

10. DESCRIPTION: The front changer has a metal cage which moves the chain from sprocket to sprocket. The cage is attached to a horizontal or diagonal pole. On some old models, the pole goes into a box or closed tube where its end is pushed to the left by a spring. Most modern, improved changers have the cage attached to a movable parallelogram gadget like the

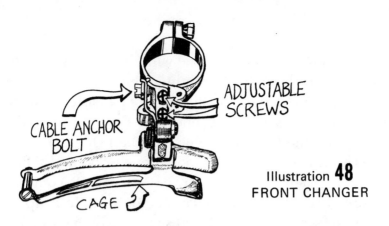

CABLE ANCHOR BOLT

ADJUSTABLE SCREWS

CAGE

Illustration **48**
FRONT CHANGER

one in Illustration 48. A spring usually pushes the side of the parallelogram so the cage goes to the left or into the low gear position. When you pull the gear lever, the cable pulls at the anchor bolt and moves the cage to the right or into the high gear position. A couple of oddball modern derailleurs are reversed; the spring pushes to the right, the cable pulls the cage left or into low gear.

PROBLEMS: *Rubbing.* The cage of the front changer rubs against one side or the other of the chain and makes a bothersome noise. First, try to eliminate the noise with the control lever. Shifting the rear changer often necessitates adjustment of the front changer. Make sure that the adjustable bolt on the control lever [see *Control Lever Problems*] is tight enough. Still got rubbing? Check alignment next. Put the bike up on a rack, get your head above the front changer, and crank the pedals slowly, watching the chain where it goes through the cage of the changer. You may notice a wobble in your sprocket. If so, go to *Front Sprocket Problems.* If the chain hits because it is running at a very sharp angle from the front to rear sprockets, see *sprocket alignment* on page 181. The next thing to check for is a misaligned changer. Are the sides of the cage parallel with the front sprockets? [See Illustration 48] Are the sides of the cage vertical?

If the whole cage isn't parallel with the front sprockets, loosen (c-cl) the bolts that tighten the changer bracket around the seat tube of the bike. (The easiest bolt to locate and loosen is the one that goes through the bracket on the *left side* of the seat tube.) Don't take the bolts all the way out—just loosen one or both of them. The Campagnolo T wrench, or Y tool will come in handy here. When the bracket is loose, slide it up or down the seat tube until it is at such a level that it holds the changer with the outer side of the cage about ¼ inch above the large front sprocket. Align the changer so that the *outer* side of the cage is exactly parallel with the front sprockets. Tighten (cl) the bolts that hold the changer to the bike frame and check the alignment from above again. Sometimes the tightening of those bolts will take the changer out of alignment. If it does, loosen them and try again, until the changer is properly aligned. If the sides of the cage aren't vertical, get out your crescent wrench and put it on the faulty side, clamping the jaws firmly. Then straighten the cage gently.

If the *aligned and straightened cage still rubs,* you have to adjust its lateral position. See how many adjustable screws there are on the body of the changer [see Illustration 48]. If there is one, you have to adjust the position of the cage on the pole that goes into the changer body. If there are two adjustable screws, skip the next paragraph and do your adjustment as described in the paragraph that follows.

On changers with one adjustable screw, the cage is held to the pole by an adjusting bolt that can be tightened at any point on the pole. Find the adjusting bolt. On some models, the bolt is very inaccessible. You will have to get at it with a Y tool or some other socket tool.

Put the chain on the smallest front sprocket, with the changer if you can make it work, or with your fingers if necessary. Push the front changer control lever all the way forward. Put the rear changer in the biggest sprocket position (lowest gear). Loosen (c-cl) the adjusting bolt that holds the front changer cage to the pole. Now move the cage laterally to the position where the innermost side is just clearing the chain. When the lateral position of the cage is right, look at the cage from the side. Make sure its curving lower edge is parallel to the curve of the sprocket, then tighten (cl) the adjusting bolt. Go easy on it. They tend to shear off. Crank the pedals to make sure there is no rub. Now put the rear changer in the smallest sprocket (highest gear) position. Pull the control lever for the front changer all the way back. Crank the pedals. Is there any nasty rubbing on either of the sides of the cage? If the outer side of the cage hits the chain, find the adjustable screw on the box or arm, and loosen (c-cl) it three or four turns to give you some slack. Put the front changer control lever in such a position that the outer side of the cage just clears the chain. Now tighten the adjustable screw up gently until it meets some resistance. That will mean that it is stopping the pole where you want it. On many changers, the point of the adjustable screw is visible. Watch it closely as you tighten (cl) the screw, and stop tightening when the point rests on the changer pivot. When the screw is right, try shifting the front changer with the rear changer in different positions. Have you taken care of the rubbing? Good. Chain throwing now? Bad. See *Chain throwing* below.

If your front changer has *two adjustable screws* on a parallelogram-shaped changer body, your *adjustment* procedure is very simple. Put the bike in its lowest possible gear (small front sprocket, biggest rear sprocket). Figure out which screw controls the inward range of the cage (one of the tips of the screws will be closer to hitting the changer body), and adjust that screw so that the innermost side of the cage barely clears the chain. Then put the bike in the highest possible gear, and adjust the other screw so that the outer side of the cage barely clears the chain.

Chain throwing, or *changer won't shift chain.* When you shift the front changer, the chain falls off the sprocket, or won't shift off it, or gets tangled in the pedals, or catches in the tire and brings you to a grinding halt. Most unpleasant. First check the *alignment* of the changer and the *adjustment* of the cage as in *Rubbing* above, and make sure that when the changers are in highest gear position (big front sprocket, littlest rear sprocket) and lowest gear position, the sides of the front changer cage are *barely* missing the cage. If the cage can move either too far out or too far in, it will throw the chain. If your problem is a chain that always throws off the big sprocket when you try to shift to it, and no amount of adjusting will stop the problem, put your crescent wrench on the front tip of the outer side of the cage, and bend it in very slightly, about 1/16 inch. This slightly bent-in cage tip will catch a chain that has throwing tendencies.

If your adjusted front changer can't get the chain *onto* one of the sprockets, the cable may be either too tight or too loose. Loosen (c-cl) the anchor bolt that holds the end of it and tighten or loosen the cable, as needed. Then tighten (cl) the anchor bolt and check to make sure the changer is still adjusted right.

If your chain throws off one of the front sprockets all the time, not just when you are shifting, you might have a very old, flobby chain. See *Chain Problems.* If the chain is in good shape, the problem is the alignment of the front and rear sprockets.

10. To test *sprocket alignment,* put the bike in its lowest gear. Lean it on a wall or put it up on a rack. Kneel down next to the front wheel on the right side of the bike. Put your head way down, just to the front of the front sprockets. Sight straight through the thin space between the front sprockets back towards the rear sprockets. If you see the middle rear sprocket through the thin space, you have a beautifully aligned bike. If one of the other rear sprockets appears in the space between the front sprockets, your power train is not aligned. Aligning is tricky. You might want to have it done by a pro. But if you feel up to doing it yourself, here are some hints.

If you see a sprocket that is bigger than the middle one (a lower gear sprocket), then you have to move the front sprockets to their right, or away from the center of the frame. This can only be done properly by getting a bottom bracket axle with a longer right end. To change the axle, see *Bottom Bracket overhaul.* If you have Ashtabula cranks, there is no way you can get a longer axle.

If you see a smaller sprocket than the middle one when you sight between the front sprockets, then you have to move the rear sprockets to their right (away from the center of the rear hub). This can be done by removing the rear wheel, removing the freewheel (see the appropriate sections), and putting a thin spacer (washer) between the freewheel and the hub. Shops carry these spacers. This may in turn move the freewheel out on the hub so much that the smallest sprocket hits the bike frame. If so, you have to put a second washer around the rear axle, between the spacer (the long nut with hex sides like a locknut) and the thin locknut. Replace the rear wheel. You may find it hard to fit between the drop-outs. All those washers make a slightly unorthodox rear wheel set-up, to say the least, but the only other alternative is getting a new frame, or having a real frame pro bend your old one.

Rear Changer

(cl) means clockwise, and usually tightens a nut or bolt. (c-cl) means counterclockwise, and usually loosens.

DESCRIPTION: The thing that changes the chain from one rear sprocket to the other. It consists of a changer body and a cage with two chain rollers, one of which holds the chain tight (the tension roller) and one of which moves the chain from sprocket to sprocket (the jockey roller). There are three distinct types of rear changers. One has a box-like body with two closed sides [see Illustration 49]. A second has a changer body

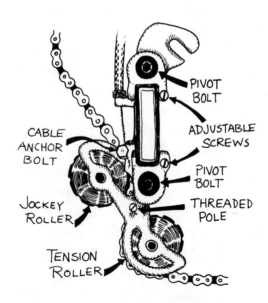

Illustration **49**
SOLID BODY CHANGER (DERAILLEUR)

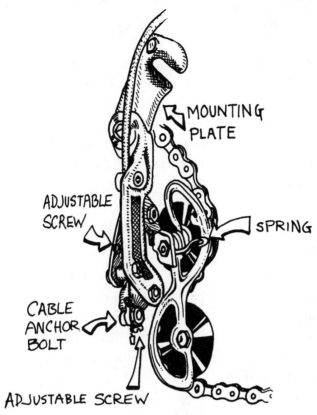

MOUNTING PLATE

ADJUSTABLE SCREW

SPRING

CABLE ANCHOR BOLT

ADJUSTABLE SCREW

Illustration **50**
SPINDLY-ARMED CHANGER (DERAILLEUR)

that is spindly, made up of thin metal arms [see Illustration 50]. The second type has some models which come with a cover over the spindly arms to hide their fragile condition. But don't be fooled. The changers with spindly-armed bodies are much more delicate than the changers with solid-walled bodies. They are much more prone to stiffness of the joints, and bent pieces that aim the chain in directions other than onto the sprockets.

The third type is the slant pantograph, exemplified by the Sun Tour model in Illustration 50a. They work great if you set them at the right angle. To do this, put the changer into the highest gear and adjust the angle screw so the changer body is parallel with the chain stay of the bike. While the changer is still in the highest gear, check the roller cage and see if it is pointing straight down at the ground, as shown. If it isn't, lengthen or shorten the chain until it is. The adjustable range screws are used as the ones on a solid body changer, and are marked with "H" and "L" for high and low; a nice touch.

There are also servo-pantograph changers. Treat them just like solid body ones; the only difference is in the angle of the dangle.

PROBLEMS: *Chain throwing* itself off, or *not making it* onto the biggest or smallest rear sprockets. Your changer needs to have its *alignment* and *adjustment* checked, at *both* the high and low ends of its range. Make sure your chain is oiled before you get into this whole procedure.

Start with *high range alignment and adjustment.* Put the bike up on a rack or stand to get the rear wheel off

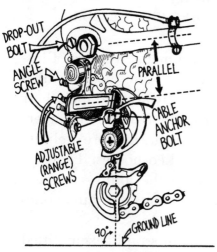

Illustration **50a**
SLANT PANTOGRAPH
CHANGER

Illustration **50b**
REAR CHANGER
ALIGNMENT

the ground, then push the control lever for the rear changer all the way forward as you pedal the cranks around. If the chain wants to throw off that small sprocket in the back, pull the control lever back a bit until it will run on the small sprocket smoothly. If the chain won't make it onto the smallest sprocket, first loosen (c-cl) the cable anchor bolt [see Illustrations 49, 50, and 50a].

Now turn the adjustable screw in or out slowly until you feel that the tip of it is in light contact with the opposing part of the changer. Turn the pedals and see that the chain is feeding smoothly onto the smallest sprocket. Whew, that's a big order. If you can't even find the little range screw, look in the illustrations. You may have one of those nice changers on which they marked the screws; in that case, look for the one with the "H". When the screw tip is touching and the chain is feeding smoothly onto the smallest sprocket, loosen (c-cl) the screw about ¼ turn. This will give the changer a bit of play so it can shift into the gear easily. Tighten (cl) the anchor bolt if you loosened it.

OK, your changer is feeding the chain onto the smallest sprocket. Now check the alignment. Get out a good straight ruler and lay it along the inside of the roller cage, so it is pointing down at the ground, as in Illustration 50b.

Is the ruler straight up and down? It should be in exactly the same plane as the rear sprockets; you can eyeball it from behind the bike. If it's in line, great, you're done with the high range and you can shift the changer a couple of times to make sure it's working, then go on to *low range alignment and adjustment* on page 188.

If the ruler is not in the same plane as the sprockets, first make sure it is flat against the side of the roller cage, not tipping up on the end of one of the bolts that go through the rollers or something. If the ruler is clearly showing that the cage is out of line, move the lower end of the ruler out or in closer to the wheel to get it in line with the sprockets. Check which way you had to move it, right here: Outward ☐   Inward ☐ You're going to have to take the changer off the bike, and you'll need to remember which way to align the mounting plate when the changer is gone. So remember not only which way you're going to bend things, but *how far* you want to make the end of that ruler move.

To do the *alignment,* remove the wheel (see page 81), then stick an Allen wrench into the pivot bolt that holds the changer to the mounting plate. The mounting plate may be a part of the bike frame, or it may be a separate piece, as is shown in Illustrations 49, 50, and 50a. Hold the pivot bolt still with the Allen wrench and loosen (c-cl) the nut that is on the other side of the plate. Use a wrench that fits well; those thin nuts get rounded off easily. When the nut is off, unscrew the pivot bolt, or, if it isn't screwed into the plate, just let the spring tension loose and pull the thing straight out. Watch for little washers and rings around that pivot bolt. Keep them on it if you can, or set them down in order the way they came off, so you'll be able to put them back together right later. If the mounting plate for your rear changer is a separate piece, loosen (c-cl) the little bolt that holds it in the drop-out, take the plate off the bike, remove the little bolt all the way, then stick the plate into one end of a sturdy vise. Slide it in until the vise is gripping all around the U-shaped slot, but not so far that the jaws crush the little bump that's pressed into the plate. [See Illustration 51]

When the plate is held either in a vise or on the bike, put a big adjustable wrench, like the Ford wrench or a 12 inch crescent or something (*not* your little 6 inch crescent) over the pivot bolt hole, as shown in Illustration 51. *Think* before you bend. Which way did you want to move it? How much? Put the ruler on the plate right now, to refresh your memory. If the thing has been taken off the bike, turned upside down, and stuck in a vise, you're going to have to think that much harder to make sure you bend it the right way. And go easy with the bending. If you do it too much and have to bend the thing back, it will weaken the metal.

So check the plate with the ruler to make sure you don't bend it too much. When you've got it right, or as close as you can tell by eyeball, put the plate and changer back on the bike. Get the washers onto the pivot bolt as they were before. If the pivot bolt has no spring tension on it, tighten it (cl), back it off (c-cl) a quarter turn, then tighten the locknut as you hold the bolt still. If there is a spring on the bolt, make sure the ends of it are in their little slots or holes, then push the bolt through the plate, spin the nut on by hand, tighten (cl) the bolt ½ turn with the Allen key and hold it there while you tighten the nut (cl) with a wrench that fits well.

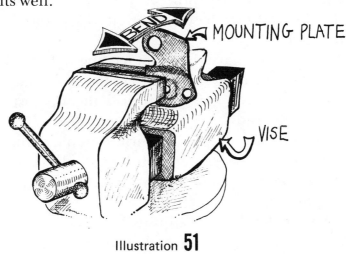

Illustration **51**

Put the wheel back on (see page 84), making sure the chain is back on the smallest sprocket, then check first with the ruler, and finally by pedaling and shifting gears, to see if the alignment is right. You should be able to get the chain into and out of the highest gear with ease. If not, try a little adjustment with the high adjustable screw, then check the following possible problems: a sticky cable (see *cable replacement*), a sticky changer (see *changer stickies*), or misaligned sprockets.

To check the changer's *low range alignment and adjustment*, first make sure the high range is OK, as above, then shift the lever back so the chain goes onto the biggest of the rear sprockets. What's that? The chain goes into the spokes, or it won't even make it onto the biggest sprocket? Tough luck. If the chain has jammed itself into the spokes, hold the wheel still from behind the bike and pull the chain up out of where it's stuck, starting at the front of the sprocket and working back around it. Yuch! When you've got the chain free, fiddle with the control lever until the chain will feed onto the biggest sprocket. If the changer can't quite get the chain up onto that sprocket, you have to loosen (c-cl) the "low" adjustable screw until it will let the chain get on there.

When you have the chain feeding onto the biggest sprocket smoothly, tighten (cl) the "low" adjustable screw until you can see or feel the tip just nudge against the resistance of the changer body. Then back the screw off (c-cl) about ¼ turn. Run the changer into and out of the lowest gear. If it goes a little rough, or if you hear a plunk-plunk-plunking of the changer tapping on the spokes, *stop pedaling.* Make sure you have the "low" screw adjusted right, then do a ruler check as you did in the high gear. This time, though, put the ruler flat on the *outer* side of the roller cage, and aim it more or less toward the front of the bike, so it is close to horizontal. Look down on the ruler from above and see if it is in the same plane as the rear sprockets. This is tricky, because the chain will be going at a slight angle toward the front sprockets, and it will distract you, making you think the ruler is pointing inward, even if it's straight. Concentrate on lining up the ruler with one of the rear sprockets. Try to ignore that chain. You might even take it off the front sprockets if that makes it easier. When you've gotten a good eyeball on the ruler, you have to make a hard choice, especially if it looks like the changer is bent out of alignment.

If the changer is bent, you can either take it to a shop with an ace mechanic for alignment, or get a new changer and put it on (much the easiest way out), or try to align the thing yourself. Alignment is very difficult and can cause trouble if you bend the drop-out instead of the mounting plate in the process. I say get a new changer or leave the aligning to a hotshot. If you're dead set on doing it yourself, use the same general procedure as for the high range alignment, but be careful. On bikes that have the mounting plate built into the drop-out, it's very easy to twist the drop-out and wreck the alignment of the whole back end of the bike's frame.

When the low range of the changer is aligned, check the range screw again. If the chain is still faltering a lot when you try to put it into the lowest gear, you may have one of the following problems, listed in order of probability: a sticky changer, an old, loose, or un-oiled chain, a rusty or sticky cable, or misaligned sprockets. See the appropriate *Problem* headings as needed.

Changer *stickies*. The changer is sluggish in shifting from one sprocket to another, especially onto the smallest sprocket, and you have checked the control lever and the cable. Try a little oil first, at the joints of the changer body [see Illustration 51]. If you have a spindly-armed changer, put it in the biggest sprocket position. Get 8 and 9 mm wrenches (the Campagnolo T wrench and the Y tool are handiest) and loosen (c-cl) each of the nuts on the little bolts at the joints of the spindly arms. Then loosen (c-cl) each bolt about 1/8 turn or less, and tighten up the nuts again. This process will limber up the joints of the spindly-armed changer, and often make its action smoother.

If you have a sticky solid body changer, you can try to work oil into the joints, but beyond that, your only recourse is to replace the sticky changer. This isn't an expensive replacement if the changer is one of those great nylon models, or the Japanese model, but if you have a fancy Italian changer, you may want to take it to a shop for a checkup before you invest in a replacement.

Chain loose, or feeding roughly. Either your chain sags when the rear changer is in the high gear positions, or your changer does not shift smoothly, and grindy chain noises often appear. First check the chain [see *Chain Problems*]. Next, take a good look at the changer, especially the chain rollers and their cage. Are the rollers covered with gunk? Is the pivot of the cage all gunked up? You may need to clean the rollers and the cage. Take them apart slowly and carefully, making sure you memorize the order of the little sleeves and washers around the pivot bolts, and making sure you don't lose any ball bearings. Oil each roller with the lubricant you use on your chain, and reassemble it, leaving plenty of play for the ball bearings if you have them. If the rollers are always getting dirty and sticky, you can get a pair of rollers made with sealed bearings, by Bullseye. They're available from catalogs, and although they cost a pile, they last forever, so they're worth it.

If the cage and rollers are not only dirty but bent out of shape, so the chain runs cockeyed, don't try to bend it back straight again; you'll just get it all sticky in its joints. See *Changer replacement,* below.

If there is a spring that you can see hooked onto the roller cage, is it broken? If so, replace it. If the part of the changer that holds the spring is banged up, replace the whole changer.

Has the spring come loose or unhooked? Reset it carefully with pliers. Don't let it nip you in the process. If you can't see any tension spring on your changer, it's probably inside a cylinder around the lower pivot bolt, the bolt that holds the roller cage.

To tighten this hidden spring, you have to loosen whatever's holding it in place, then tighten the spring, then tighten the holder. Start by removing any cap that is on the end of the pivot bolt. When the cap is off, you'll see either a "castellated" bolt end under there (as on the Sun Tour changer, for instance) or a simple hex-shaped hole for an Allen wrench.

If there's a castellated bolt (one that looks like the turret of a castle), you just take off (c-cl) the little threaded pole on the cage, spin the cage (cl) until it is loose, then move the hook end of the spring from one slot in that turret thing to the next slot in a counter-clockwise direction. Now wind the spring back up, put the threaded pole back in (cl) and screw the cap back in (cl) to hold the whole works together.

If you have a hex-hole in the end of your pivot bolt, put an Allen key in it and hold it still, then undo (c-cl) the nut or the cage itself at the other end of the pivot bolt. You may need to undo (c-cl) a threaded pole if you want to turn the whole cage around, and you may have to take off the tension roller and remove the chain for the same purpose.

Keep holding that pivot bolt for a moment, so the spring doesn't go loose, then figure out how you can tighten the spring. It can be done in lots of different ways, depending on the changer. If there is a locknut right next to the cage, as on the Simplex changer, loosen the cage and the locknut (c-cl), then turn the pivot bolt (c-cl) so the spring tightens, then tighten the locknut against the cage (cl). On other changers you have to take the cage off and turn it clockwise so the end of the spring can fit into a different little hole which will bring up the tension when the whole thing is put back together. On some models, the only thing you can do is turn the whole cage once counterclockwise and then put the threaded pole back in. This will make the spring really tight, so be careful. Tighten up the cage or nut on the pivot bolt when the spring is tight, no matter which set-up you have.

Changer replacement is a *good* alternative to overhaul and alignment, if you can afford it. Any bent changer, or changer with corners and edges knocked off, should be replaced. Start by removing the rear wheel. Loosen (c-cl) the cable anchor bolt and remove the cable. Unscrew (c-cl) the little bolt that holds the changer mounting plate in the drop-out, if you have one, and take the whole changer and plate off the bike frame. If you have a changer which is bolted directly into a hole in the drop-out, unscrew (c-cl) the bolt, and take the changer off. Undo (c-cl) one of the roller bolts and remove the roller to release the chain from the roller cage. Take the changer to a good shop and get a new one. I recommend the solid body models. Put the plate of the new changer (or the mounting bolt, if yours is the direct bolt-on type) into the drop-out, and tighten (cl) the mounting bolt. If the mounting bolt has a nut that goes on the back of the mounting plate, spin the nut on, loosen (c-cl) the mounting pivot bolt about ¼ turn, then hold it still with the Allen key while you tighten (cl) the nut back behind the plate. Take the tension roller (the lower one) out, loop the chain over it, and replace it so that the chain makes a reverse S through the rollers. Tighten (cl) the roller bolt up again. If the roller has ball bearings, check to make sure that the roller turns freely without being so loose that it wobbles. Adjust the two cones (cl is tighter, c-cl is looser) as needed. Connect the cable to the cable anchor bolt, and adjust the range-limiting screws so that the changer shifts smoothly into the largest and smallest sprockets without throwing the chain [see *Chain throwing*].

Appendix-Vestiges

Anything on a bicycle that isn't absolutely essential to its function is vestigial. Extra. Dead weight.

Some extras, which I will list first, can be worth their weight. The others make me feel like I have appendicitis if I write about them, so I refuse to say much at all.

Toe clips. The little metal frames with leather straps that attach to the pedals and hold your feet in place. These are a must for long-distance riding. They make it easier for a rider to keep an even pace, and they save all the energy he would waste trying to keep his feet in place on the pedals. There are different sizes. Get ones to fit you, and make sure they are bolted on well.

Helmet. A must for any serious cycling, especially in traffic. There are several different high-quality cycling helmets. Any good skating or other sport helmet will help, but consider chipping in for a real good one; heads are one to a customer.

Mud guards (fenders). A very useful vestige when it's raining. Make sure they are bolted well at all brace ends. If the braces rub the wheel, loosen (c-cl) the bolts that hold them to the frame and adjust, then retighten (cl) the bolts. That's better than bending the braces out like wishbones. For extra water protection, glue or tape pie-shaped pieces of plastic sheathing from the drop-outs to the mud guard between the braces. These pieces are most needed at the back of the front wheel and the front of the back wheel.

Carrier. One common variety which I recommend is the aluminum Pletscher one. It fits behind the seat, over the rear wheel. It has a spring clamp. Make sure all bolts and nuts for it are kept tight. You can get a clever, lightweight "rack support" for your carrier from many catalogs and stores. It will keep the carrier from slipping down onto your brakes. You can also get all kinds of other fancy racks and things for your bike. I don't like that stuff. I have a 3 speed with a big basket for shopping. If I have to carry a little something when I'm riding my lightweight bike, I use a little cloth rucksack, which I fold up and put into my pocket after I've eaten the little something. That rules out camping on a bike for me.

Pump. For sew-up people, a good, solid one is a must. For all others, the pumps that fit on the bike are usually inadequate. Get a good hand pump for your garage, or use the gas station air carefully, making sure not to over-inflate.

Water bottle. The plastic kind that fits in a little wire cage that's clamped to the frame. Only needed on long, dry rides. On *very* long, dry rides, you may need two or even three bottles.

Kickstand. Make sure the bolt (if there is one) that holds it tight between the chain-stays is *extra* tight. If your stand is a little too long for your bike (the bike stands up too straight and falls over easily), try leaning the bike on the stand, then picking up the rear wheel 3 inches so the weight of the bike is on the stand. Now push down from straight above the stand so that it bends until the rear wheel comes back to earth. Bike leaning over more? It should be. If your crank hits the kickstand, loosen (c-cl) the bolt that holds the stand, move the stand, and tighten (cl) the bolt well.

Light. There is only one kind I use and recommend. The cheap little French arm-band light. Strap it to your leg just below the knee so it bobs up and down when you pedal. It might save your life. Other lights with generators, batteries, wires, directional signals, toggle switches and other such vestigial crap are not only unaesthetic—they are dangerous because they get caught in things, and they usually don't work. If you find night riding without a headlight spooky, stick to daytime riding. Simple enough?

Lock. The best lock is the human eye. If you have a good bike, take it inside with you, or lock it to something outside a window that you can keep glancing through. Keep your eye on it. Don't leave a good bike locked with any lock outside overnight. Oh, jeez, I get bad vibes talking about locks. I'll never get over having my dear old Cinelli ripped off. Put it this way. If you steal bikes, for God's sake, stop it. If you steal a bike from someone who loves it and depends on it, you are doing one of the lowest things that one human being can do to another. Steal something else if you have to steal.

Chain guards. Hard to keep from hitting on them with the crank and other things, isn't it? I agree. If yours is troublesome, take it off, and put a rubber band or a pants clip around your cuff.

Brake lever extensions, raccoon tails, streamers, "chopper" forks, "sissy" bars, chromed tailpipes, imitation leopard skin banana seats. Filth, Filth. Filth and junk. I refuse to say more about them.

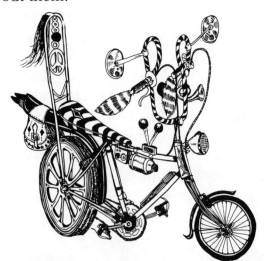

Postscript

This isn't the end. Tomorrow I'll probably find some problem I haven't covered in this book. Or, more likely, *you* will find something I didn't cover well enough. If you do, write to me about it so I can make this book better in the future. I hope there will always be two more bicycle problems—one that I can tinker with, and one that you can tinker with.

Write: Tom Cuthbertson, c/o the publisher.

Index

a

b

c

TWO OTHER BOOKS BY TOM CUTHBERTSON
AND ILLUSTRATED BY RICK MORRALL

ANYBODY'S SKATEBOARD BOOK

Anybody's Skateboard Book is a lively introduction to the sport of skateboarding. It tells the novice how to get a first skateboard and how to use it safely, and it details all of the different possible activities now open to skateboarders. Downhill riding, freestyle tricks and radical riding techniques are covered thoroughly, and there is a section on skateboard repairs and adjustments.
6x9" 142 pages $3 paper, $7.95 cloth

BIKE TRIPPING

Bike Tripping is an enjoyable and thorough guide to the world of bicycles. Find out what equipment you will need. Learn to ride and how to plan short trips and long hauls. Special sections provide information on safety, choosing your route, and transporting your bike to the starting point.
6x9" 185 pages $3.95 paper, $7.95 cloth

At your local book store, or order directly from

TEN SPEED PRESS
Box 7123, Berkeley, California 94707
Please include 50¢ additional for paperback, or 75¢ additional for clothbound, to cover cost of postage and handling.